BrightRED Study Guide

CfE ADVANCED Higher
MUSIC

Adrian Finnerty

First published in 2023 by:
Mitchelston Drive Business Centre
Mitchelston Drive
Kirkcaldy
KY1 3NB

Copyright © Bright Red Publishing Ltd 2023

Cover image © Caleb Rutherford

All rights reserved. No part of this publication may be reproduced, stored in a retrieval system, or transmitted in any form or by any means, electronic, mechanical, photocopying, recording or otherwise, without prior permission in writing from the publisher.

The rights of Adrian Finnerty to be identified as the author of this work have been asserted by them in accordance with Sections 77 and 78 of the Copyright, Designs and Patents Act 1988.

A CIP record for this book is available from the British Library.

ISBN 978-1-84948-351-3

With thanks to:
PDQ Digital Media Solutions Ltd, Bungay (layout), Philippa Tomlinson (copy-edit).
Cover design and series book design by Caleb Rutherford – e i d e t i c.

Acknowledgements
Every effort has been made to seek all copyright-holders. If any have been overlooked, then Bright Red Publishing will be delighted to make the necessary arrangements.

Permission has been sought from all relevant copyright holders and Bright Red Publishing are grateful for the use of the following:

Image credits
carlos castilla/Shutterstock.com (p 4 top); Shyntartanya/Shutterstock.com (p 4 bottom); ngupakarti/Shutterstock.com (p 6 top); wjarek/Shutterstock.com (p 6 bottom); Kraft74/Shutterstock.com (p 7 middle); Vladimir Hodac/Shutterstock.com (p 7 bottom); Dm_Cherry/Shutterstock.com (p 8); Valery Sidelnykov/Shutterstock.com (p 9 top); spatuletail/Shutterstock.com (p 9 bottom); NaxosUSA/Shutterstock.com (p 10); Tim Mainiero/Shutterstock.com (p 11); Olga Popova/Shutterstock.com (p 12); mongione/Shutterstock.com (p 13); abstract/Shutterstock.com (p 14); Scott Rothstein/Shutterstock.com (p 18 top); Morphart Creation/Shutterstock.com (p 20 top); three images by Morphart Creation/Shutterstock.com (p 20 top & bottom, p 22); Uncle Leo/Shutterstock.com (p 23); frantic00/Shutterstock.com (p 24); Ivan Yohan/Shutterstock.com (p 28); Mo Wu/Shutterstock.com (p 30); Kraft74/Shutterstock.com (p 31); Yuri Gurevich/Shutterstock.com (p 36); Everett Collection/Shutterstock.com (p 38); Chad McDermott/Shutterstock.com (p 40 top); DaLiu/Shutterstock.com (p 40 bottom); Prachaya Roekdeethaweesab/Shutterstock.com (p 48); OSABEE/Shutterstock.com (p 50); Chinnapong/Shutterstock.com (p 62); Rawpixel.com/Shutterstock.com (p 63); INSAGO/Shutterstock.com (p 66); Wongsiri Subhayon/Shutterstock.com (p 70–71); Ground Picture/Shutterstock.com (p 76); Brian Goodman/Shutterstock.com (p 78); Stmool/Shutterstock.com (p 79); PeopleImages.com – Yuri A/Shutterstock.com (p 82); New Africa/Shutterstock.com (p 84 left); two images by Yulia Glam/Shutterstock.com (p 84, 86, 90 middle & right); Luca Lorenzelli/Shutterstock.com (p 86 bottom); Labutin.Art/Shutterstock.com (p 88 top); 9dream studio/Shutterstock.com (p 88 bottom); Gorodenkoff/Shutterstock.com (p 89 top); Soloviova Liudmyla/Shutterstock.com (p 89 bottom); VisualArtStudio/Shutterstock.com (p 92).

Music credits
Lyrics to 'Bell Anthem' by Purcell and 'Zadok the Priest' by Handel – scripture quotations from The Authorized (King James) Version. Rights in the Authorized Version in the United Kingdom are vested in the Crown. Reproduced by permission of the Crown's patentee, Cambridge University Press (pp 20–21); English translation of Bach's 'Wachet auf, ruft uns die Stimme' by Francis Browne, taken from www.bach-cantatas.com/Texts/Chorale172-Eng3.htm. Reproduced by permission of Francis Browne (pp 24–25); 'America' © Copyright 1956, 1957, 1958, 1959 by Amberson Holdings LLC and Stephen Sondheim. Copyright renewed. Leonard Bernstein Music Publishing Company LLC, publisher. Boosey & Hawkes, agent for rental. International copyright secured. Reproduced by permission of Boosey & Hawkes Music Publishers Ltd. (p 31); 'Cool' © Copyright 1956, 1957, 1958, 1959 by Amberson Holdings LLC and Stephen Sondheim. Copyright renewed. Leonard Bernstein Music Publishing Company LLC, publisher. Boosey & Hawkes, agent for rental. International copyright secured. Reproduced by permission of Boosey & Hawkes Music Publishers Ltd. (p 34); 'Intermezzo' from Háry János by Zoltán Kodály © 1927 Universal Edition A.G. Wien. Reproduced by permission. All rights reserved (p 41); 'Gavotta' by Prokofieff © Copyright 1926 by Hawkes & Son (London) Ltd. (p 47); 'Sinfonia (Overture)' by Stravinsky © Copyright 1924 by Hawkes & Son (London) Ltd. Revised version: © Copyright 1949 by Hawkes & Son (London) Ltd. U.S. Copyright renewed. Reproduced by permission of Boosey & Hawkes Music Publishers Ltd (p 47); 'Petrushka' by Stravinsky © Copyright 1912 by Hawkes & Son (London) Ltd. Revised version: © Copyright 1912 by Hawkes & Son (London) Ltd. U.S. Copyright renewed. Reproduced by permission of Boosey & Hawkes Music Publishers Ltd. (pp 48–9); 'Three Pieces for String Quartet' by Stravinsky © Copyright 1923 by Hawkes & Son (London) Ltd. (p 49); 'Take Five' by Paul Desmond © 1960 Derry Music Company (world excluding United States), Desmond Music Company (United States) (p 59).

Printed and bound in the UK.

CONTENTS

INTRODUCTION

Course overview.................................4

MUSIC CONCEPTS

Contemporary jazz and electronic dance music (EDM)...6
Vocal music....................................8
Song cycle 1..................................10
Song cycle 2..................................12
Sacred music – mass..........................14
Sacred music – motet.........................16
Sacred music – anthem 1......................18
Sacred music – anthem 2......................20
Sacred music – chorale 1.....................22
Sacred music – chorale 2.....................24
Renaissance vocal music......................26
Renaissance instrumental and dance music.....28
Antiphonal texture...........................30
Fugue..32
Chorale fugues...............................34
Piano trio...................................36
Leitmotif....................................38

MUSIC STYLES

Nationalist music............................40
Serial music 1...............................42
Serial music 2...............................44
Neoclassical music...........................46
Bitonality and polytonality..................48

MUSIC LITERACY

Concepts.....................................50
Scales and key signatures....................52
Chords and inversions........................54
More chords and intervals....................56
Rhythm.......................................58
Signs, symbols and abbreviations.............60

COURSE ASSESSMENT

Course overview..............................62
The Question paper 1.........................64
The Question paper 2.........................66
The Question paper 3.........................68
Some helpful tips............................70
Identifying prominent concepts and analysis 1........72
Identifying prominent concepts and analysis 2........74

ASSIGNMENT

Overview and composing review................76
Composing....................................78
Arranging....................................80
The composing or arranging process...........82
Assessment of composing......................84
Assessment of arranging......................86
Score or performance plan....................88
Review of the creative process...............90
Analysing music..............................92

APPENDICES

Glossary.....................................94
Index..97

INTRODUCTION

COURSE OVERVIEW

INTRODUCTION

The aims of the Advanced Higher Music course overall are to enable you to:

- broaden your knowledge and understanding of music and music literacy by listening to music, analysing and identifying music concepts, and identifying signs and symbols used in music notation
- create original music or arrange existing music, using compositional methods, and self-reflect on your creative choices
- perform music on at least one instrument or voice, and self-reflect on your progress.

Throughout the Advanced Higher Music course, you will further develop a range of musical skills, knowledge and understanding to an advanced level. These include:

- skills in listening to music to promote aural perception and discrimination
- knowledge and understanding of music styles and concepts, as well as signs and symbols in music notation
- analysing music
- creating original music or arranging existing music using compositional methods
- reviewing the creative process of composing and/or arranging
- performing music in contrasting styles on one instrument, two contrasting instruments, or one instrument and voice
- self-reflection and review of your rehearsal and practice skills.

COURSE CONTENT

The Advanced Higher Music course has an integrated approach to learning about music. It combines practical activities in performing and composing (and/or arranging) with music literacy and listening to music. Learning about music concepts is central to the course. Through listening to a wide range of music you will deepen your understanding of a variety of music styles and concepts, as well as extending your knowledge of signs and symbols used in music notation.

Throughout the course, you will have opportunities to draw on your understanding of music styles and concepts as you experiment with these in creative ways when performing and creating music. You will develop performing skills on one instrument or voice through regular practice and reflection on your progress. You also have the choice of one of the following options:

- Performance option – performing on a second, contrasting, instrument or voice
- Portfolio option – composing a portfolio of music.

Advanced Higher Music concepts

The music concepts are all the styles, music features and terms that you will learn about as part of your Advanced Higher Music course. You will explore these concepts in a variety of ways through listening to music, creating your own music and performing music.

The concepts at Advanced Higher level build on previous knowledge and understanding of music concepts at lower levels. This means that you will be expected to have a secure understanding of the music concepts from National 3, National 4, National 5 and Higher levels, in addition to knowledge and understanding of the Advanced Higher music concepts.

The tables on page 5 list all the concepts that are introduced at Advanced Higher level. The concepts for National 3, National 4 and National 5 Music can be found in the *Bright Red National 5 Music Study Guide*, and all the concepts for Higher level can be found in the *Bright Red Higher Music Study Guide*.

> **DON'T FORGET**
>
> You have a choice between performing on two instruments or one instrument and voice, or performing on one instrument or voice and submitting a portfolio of compositions and/or arrangements.

contd

Introduction: Course overview

Advanced Higher Music concepts

Styles	Melody/harmony	Rhythm/tempo	Texture/structure/form	Timbre
Renaissance Pavan Galliard Motet Ayre or air Ballett Madrigal Anthem Chorale Nationalist Neoclassical Serial Contemporary jazz Electronic dance music (EDM)	Appoggiatura Turn Tritone Augmented triad Suspension Chords I, IV, V and VI in major and minor keys Chord II and its first inversion (major keys only) Polytonality or bitonality Tone row or note row	Hemiola	Fugue Subject Answer Countersubject Stretto Antiphonal Bridge Song cycle Leitmotif Inversion Retrograde	Consort Countertenor Piano trio Sprechgesang

Advanced Higher Music literacy

Melody/harmony	Rhythm/tempo
Bass clef C–E two ledger lines below stave to two ledger lines above Transposing from bass clef one octave higher into treble clef Rewriting (in either treble or bass clef) a note at the same pitch using up to two ledger lines below or above the stave Enharmonic equivalent — rewriting a note at the same pitch Scales and key signatures — D major, B flat major, E minor and D minor 1st and 2nd inversions of major and minor triads in the keys of C, G, F, D and B flat major and A, E and D minor Chord II and its 1st inversion (major keys as listed above) Identifying chords at cadence points and under melodies Inserting chords at cadence points Creating a bass line using chord information provided Diminished 7th Dominant 7th Added 6th Augmented triad Tritone Augmented 4th Diminished 5th *8va* (octave higher); *8vb* (octave lower)	Ties Syncopated rhythms Time signature: 5/4 Time changes Dal segno (D.S.) *Fine*

DON'T FORGET

For Advanced Higher Music, you will also need to know all the music concepts from National 3, National 4, National 5 and Higher levels.

You will notice that there are no additional music literacy concepts introduced in the **texture/structure/form** or **dynamics/timbre** categories at Advanced Higher level. However, do remember that you will still be expected to demonstrate a knowledge and understanding of music literacy concepts in these categories from lower levels.

The tables can be used as a checklist of the Advanced Higher concepts you need to know. You could highlight the concepts, choosing a different colour for each theme or topic. This will also help you to identify all the concepts that you already know, and let you see which concepts you might not be so sure of. You might find it helpful to create a mind map for each music style or topic that you study, showing which concepts relate to one another.

 THINGS TO DO AND THINK ABOUT

Remember to:

- reflect regularly on your performing progress
- review and evaluate your composing and/or arranging
- revise both the music concepts and the music literacy concepts.

MUSIC CONCEPTS

CONTEMPORARY JAZZ AND ELECTRONIC DANCE MUSIC (EDM)

You will already have studied a number of popular music styles as part of National 5 and Higher Music. For Advanced Higher Music there are two additional popular music styles that you need to be aware of – **contemporary jazz** and **electronic dance music (EDM)**.

DON'T FORGET

If you want to revise popular music styles from previous levels, you can refer to the Bright Red N5 and Higher music study guides, and also go to www.brightredbooks.net/subjects.

DON'T FORGET

A riff is a repeated musical phrase found in various styles of popular music.

DON'T FORGET

Cross rhythms occur when contrasting rhythms are played against each other.

ONLINE

Go to the Digital Zone and click the link to listen to *In The Crease* at www.brightredbooks.net/subjects.

CONTEMPORARY JAZZ

Contemporary jazz is a general term covering various styles of jazz music from about the 1980s onwards; including *jazz fusion* (a combination of jazz, rock and funk), *pop jazz* (jazz interpretations of pop songs), *crossover* (including elements of rhythm and blues) and *smooth jazz* (a blend of jazz fusion and easy-listening pop).

Common features of contemporary jazz

Melody

Melodies are generally extended improvisations which are very chromatic, often developed from repeated motifs or short phrases.

Harmony

Harmonies tend to be very rich and chromatic, often with discords, sometimes sounding impressionistic or atonal.

Rhythm/tempo

Rhythms are generally complex, with syncopation, cross rhythms and time changes. The tempo is often fast.

Texture/structure/form

Many pieces are developed from the repetition of short melodic or rhythmic figures, or based on a riff consisting of just two or three chords.

Timbre

Some of the instruments used, such as piano, saxophone, drum kit and double bass, are common to other styles of jazz. However, amplified instruments such as electric guitar (sometimes using different effects), bass guitar and keyboards are also common. There might also be other instruments not commonly found in jazz, such as the flute, oboe or flugelhorn. Instruments are sometimes played in unusual or experimental ways, exploring a range of tonal qualities such as harsh percussive sounds or harmonics.

ACTIVITY:

In The Crease by the Branford Marsalis Quartet is performed by a tenor saxophone, piano, double bass and drum kit. The music starts with the tenor saxophone playing a repeated motif which is developed throughout the piece. The piano and double bass provide an accompaniment based on riffs, with the piano also playing discords, while the drum kit plays complex rhythm patterns.

The saxophone continues with an extended improvised solo, which is very chromatic. The tone is also quite harsh at times. There is then an extended improvised solo from the piano, containing many complex runs and percussive-sounding discords. The double bass and drum kit continue to provide a sophisticated rhythmic backing as the music increases in intensity.

The tempo then slows down slightly as the saxophone returns with same motif from the beginning. This final section features an extended riff played by the saxophone, piano and double bass, while the drum kit plays a series of complex cross rhythms. The whole piece ends abruptly.

The Branford Marsalis Quartet

contd

Music concepts: Contemporary jazz and electronic dance music (EDM)

ELECTRONIC DANCE MUSIC (EDM)

Electronic dance music (often referred to by the initials **EDM**) is also known as *club music*, *dance music* or just *dance*. The term covers a range of music styles popular in the 1980s and subsequent decades, such as *house, dubstep, drum and bass, techno* and *trance*. It was aimed mainly at nightclubs, raves and festivals, where the DJ would combine tracks electronically into one smooth mix. EDM was originally created using drum machines, synthesisers and sequencers, but is now mostly produced using computers and software that contains sampling, effects and multi-track recording techniques.

Common features of EDM

The overall timbre is based on the use of electronic sounds and effects rather than acoustic instruments or voices. Sometimes the sounds are built from samples of previous recordings. While acoustic instruments and voices are used, they are often subject to production effects and processes to alter the sound. EDM often has a prominent percussion track and typically includes a melody played by a synthesiser laid over a repetitive drum beat.

ONLINE

Go online to the Digital Zone and click the link to listen to *One More Time* by Daft Punk at www.brightredbooks.net/subjects.

As the music is created specifically for dancing, there is generally a strong emphasis on rhythm and tempo. While the tempo is usually fast, there are also examples of EDM which are slower, with more ambient sounds and less emphasis on maintaining a steady beat.

ACTIVITY:

One More Time by Daft Punk contains many of the features associated with EDM. The music starts quietly with some effects, suggesting the rave is just getting underway. There is a crescendo with repeated chords and a distinct drum beat. A solo voice then comes in, with production effects altering the sound. The accompaniment features a riff using a repeated bass pattern and chords using electronic sounds. About halfway through the track the drum beat stops and the repeated chords become more ambient, possibly suggesting settling down towards the end of the evening. The vocal line is subjected to different effects and processes as the drum beat starts again and the riff continues. The music ends suddenly with the sampled sound of a clock chiming, possibly suggesting the end of the night.

DON'T FORGET

Electronic dance music (EDM) features sounds produced by synthesisers and drum machines, along with effects and processed samples from other recordings. It sounds electronic overall.

THINGS TO DO AND THINK ABOUT

Consider creating your own EDM track. There are a number of music apps, suitable for both computers and portable devices, that contain features such as creating and overlaying tracks, creating loops, using samples and adding effects and processes. You might start off by creating a drum track or a short chord sequence. You could then explore and experiment with some of the sounds available to you, including samples. You might then develop your track by adding a melody, countermelody and bass line, using some of the sounds that you like. Finally, you could further develop the timbre by adding different effects and processes to individual parts or sections.

If you choose to work with pre-recorded loops or samples, you must do so within the context of a wider composition and show the compositional process. Your own creative input must be clearly identifiable.

ONLINE TEST

To take an online test on this topic, go to the Digital Zone at www.brightredbooks.net/subjects.

7

MUSIC CONCEPTS

VOCAL MUSIC

Vocal music is any kind of music performed by one or more singers, with or without instrumental accompaniment. Concepts associated with choral music and vocal ensembles can be found in the sections on sacred music and Renaissance vocal music. In this section, the focus is on concepts associated mainly with music for solo voice. You will already have studied concepts associated with vocal music such as recitative, da capo aria, coloratura, lied, strophic and through-composed, as well as different types of voices.

DON'T FORGET

Strophic is a form in which the same music is repeated for each verse. Through-composed is a form in which there is little or no repetition from one verse to another.

ONLINE

Go to the Digital Zone and click the link to listen to *What if I never speed* at www.brightredbooks.net/subjects.

DON'T FORGET

A countertenor is a very high male voice whose vocal range is similar to that of a female alto or mezzo-soprano.

ONLINE

Go to the Digital Zone and click the link to listen to *Ombra mai fù* at www.brightredbooks.net/subjects.

AYRE

For Advanced Higher Music, the additional concepts associated with solo vocal music that you will need to be familiar with are **ayre** (or **air**), **countertenor**, **sprechgesang**, **bridge** and **song cycle**. An ayre (or air) is a type of song commonly associated with Renaissance music. It can be performed in a variety of different ways – by a solo voice or by voices singing in harmony, either a cappella or with instrumental accompaniment – but is commonly performed by a solo voice with instrumental accompaniment.

ACTIVITY:

What if I never speed by John Dowland is an example of an ayre from the Renaissance. The song is performed by a solo tenor accompanied by a viol (a bowed string instrument) and a lute (a plucked string instrument played in a similar way to the guitar). The printed music is in the key of A minor and has four beats in a bar. The texture is simply melody and accompaniment, and the word-setting is mainly syllabic. The song has two verses, both of which are in binary (AB) form. Each section ends with a perfect cadence and a tierce de Picardie. As the same music is repeated for each verse, the overall structure is strophic.

COUNTERTENOR

You will already be aware of different types of voices from studying vocal music for National 5 and Higher Music. Another type of voice that you will be expected to recognise for Advanced Higher is **countertenor**. This is an adult male voice whose vocal range is higher than that of a tenor, being similar in range to that of a female alto or mezzo-soprano. The countertenor voice is particularly popular in some Renaissance and Baroque music.

ACTIVITY:

Ombra mai fù is the opening aria from Handel's opera *Xerxes* (or *Serse*), also known as Handel's 'Largo'. The main character, admiring the shade of a plane tree, sings: 'Never was a shade of any plant dearer and more lovely, or more sweet.'

The music is in the key of D major and has three beats in the bar. Following an extended introduction of about 40 seconds – played by a small Baroque ensemble consisting of strings, harpsichord and lute – the countertenor enters with a long note.

contd

Music concepts: Vocal music

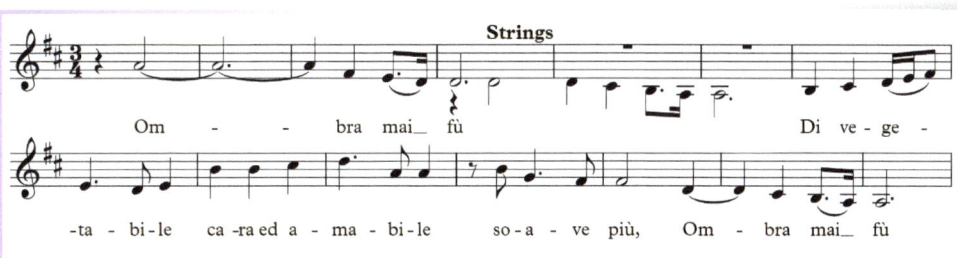

SPRECHGESANG

Sprechgesang (*speech song*) is a German term for the technique in which the vocalist is required to glide in and out of the written notes in a cross between singing and speaking.

 **ACTIVITY:**

Pierrot Lunaire (*Pierrot by Moonlight* or *Moonstruck Pierrot*) by Schönberg is a setting of twenty-one poems, by the Belgian poet Albert Giraud, for female voice and chamber ensemble. The central character is the tragicomic white-faced clown of the old French pantomime and is sometimes performed with the vocalist dressed as a clown.

The first song, *Mondestrunken* (*Moondrunk*), features the vocalist using sprechgesang. This is indicated in the music notation by small crosses through the stems of the notes. The German text translates as: 'The wine we drink with our eyes, at night pours from the moon in waves'. The instruments playing are the flute, violin (con sordino), cello and piano. The music is atonal, with many discords played on the piano. Other prominent features include time changes, trills and a polyphonic texture.

BRIDGE

A **bridge** (or **bridge passage**) is a section of music that links two main themes. In popular music, however, the term 'bridge' is often used more widely to describe a contrasting section of a song. Generally coming in the second half of a song, the bridge can be either vocal or instrumental. It often comes after two verses and choruses and provides some musical contrast before a third verse and chorus. The contrast might be a new key or chord progression, a different rhythm or tempo, or a change in instrumentation.

The song *Here Comes the Sun* by George Harrison follows a verse and chorus structure overall. After an instrumental introduction, featuring an acoustic guitar, the song starts with the chorus. Then, after two verses and choruses, the bridge starts at around 1½ minutes. The bridge is based on a different chord progression from the rest of the song. Other prominent features of the bridge include repetition, drum fills and time changes. The bridge is followed by a third verse and chorus, and the song ends with a coda.

THINGS TO DO AND THINK ABOUT

Listen to some different songs that have a bridge and consider how the bridge provides musical contrast. It might be helpful to consider the following questions when listening to the bridge.

- Are there any changes to the chord progression, key or tonality?
- Are there any changes to the rhythm or tempo?
- Are there any changes to the instrumentation?
- Are there any other prominent features in the music?

 **DON'T FORGET**

Sprechgesang is a cross between singing and speaking.

 **DON'T FORGET**

Con sordino is an Italian term indicating that the instrument is to be played with a mute.

 ONLINE

Go online to the Digital Zone to listen to *Mondestrunken* by clicking the link at www.brightredbooks.net/subjects.

 **DON'T FORGET**

The bridge is a contrasting section that generally comes around the middle of a song.

 ONLINE

Go to the Digital Zone and click the link to listen to *Here Comes the Sun* at www.brightredbooks.net/subjects.

 ONLINE

You can listen to more songs that have a bridge by clicking the links on the Digital Zone at www.brightredbooks.net/subjects.

 ONLINE TEST

To take an online test on this topic, go to the Digital Zone at www.brightredbooks.net/subjects.

MUSIC CONCEPTS

SONG CYCLE 1

During the Romantic period, composers such as Schubert and Schumann composed many examples of lieder. Sometimes they would compose a group of songs, using texts by the same writer and based on the same theme or subject, often outlining a story. A selection of songs linked together in such a way is called a **song cycle**. Well-known examples of song cycles include Schubert's *Winterreise* (*Winter Journey*) and *Die schöne Müllerin* (*The Fair Maid of the Mill*), Schumann's *Dichterliebe* (*A Poet's Love*) and *Frauenliebe und Leben* (*Woman's Love and Life*), and Beethoven's *An die ferne Geliebte* (*To the Distant Beloved*).

DON'T FORGET

A lied is a German song for voice and piano from the Romantic period. The piano accompaniment often helps to create the mood and character of the song.

Franz Schubert (1797–1828)

DON'T FORGET

Anacrusis is a note, or group of notes, that comes before the first beat of a bar.

ONLINE

Go online to the Digital Zone and click the link to listen to *Das Wandern* at www.brightredbooks.net/subjects.

SCHUBERT'S *DIE SCHÖNE MÜLLERIN* (*THE FAIR MAID OF THE MILL*)

ACTIVITY:

Schubert's *Die schöne Müllerin* (*The Fair Maid of the Mill*) is a cycle of twenty songs based on poems by Wilhelm Müller. They tell the story of a young miller who falls in love with the daughter of the mill's owner. She falls in love with a hunter, however, and rejects the miller. In despair, the miller drowns himself in a stream which had become a 'companion' to him.

In the first song, *Das Wandern* (*Wandering*), the miller expresses of his joy at wandering through the countryside, singing of the restless waters, millstones and millwheels of his profession. The music is in a major key, has two beats in a bar, and starts with a piano accompaniment featuring broken chords. The baritone voice enters with an anacrusis, while the piano continues its repetitive accompaniment, changing between broken chords and octaves. The song is in strophic form and ends with a short coda based on the same musical idea as the introduction.

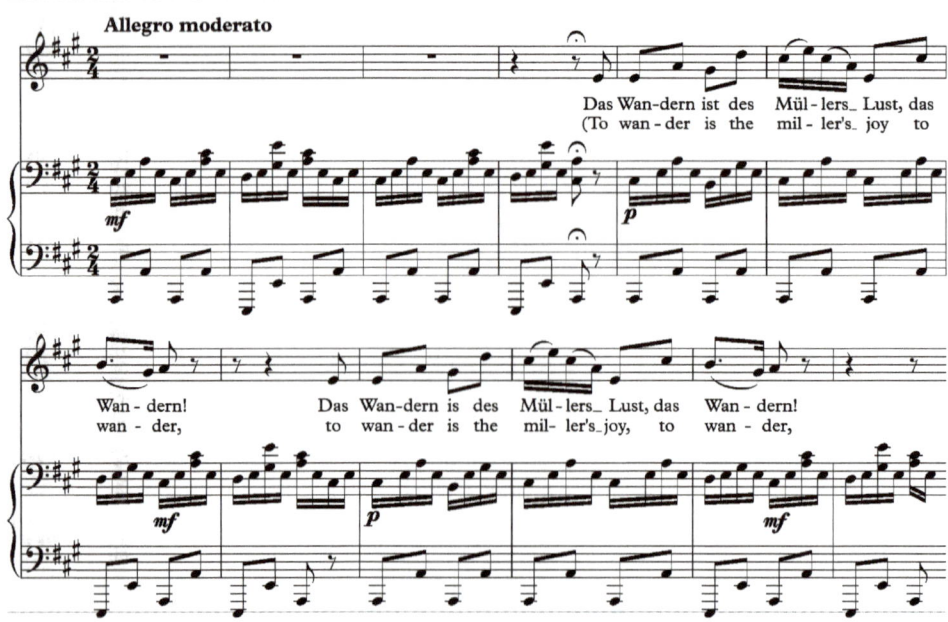

In the second song, *Wohin?* (*Whither?*), the miller comes upon a brook flowing down a hillside, which he decides to follow. The music starts with a rippling piano accompaniment featuring continuous semiquavers, suggesting the flowing water. The overall structure of the song is through-composed.

contd

Music concepts: Song cycle 1

DON'T FORGET

Through-composed is a form in which there is little or no repetition from one verse to another.

In the seventh song, *Ungedulde* (*Impatience*), the miller is impatient to tell the world of his love. The song is in strophic form and the piano plays an agitated offbeat triplet rhythm, suggesting the miller's restless state of mind.

In the fourteenth song, *Der Jäger* (*The Hunter*), the miller's rival – the hunter – appears on the scene. The music is in compound time and in strophic form, with the tonality rapidly alternating between a minor key and its relative major.

The nineteenth song, *Der Müller und der Bach* (*The Miller and the Brook*), is like a conversation between the stream and the broken-hearted miller. The gentle chordal accompaniment gives way to a broken chord pattern, as the tonality changes from minor to major. The song is in ternary form overall, ending with a coda played by the piano.

ONLINE

Go online to the Digital Zone and click the link to listen to *Wohin?* At www.brightredbooks.net/subjects.

THINGS TO DO AND THINK ABOUT

Listen to different songs from Schubert's *Die schöne Müllerin*. In each case:
- identify the structure of the song (e.g. binary, ternary, strophic or through-composed)
- consider how the piano part contributes to the overall mood and character of the song
- identify any other prominent melodic, harmonic or rhythmic concepts in the music.

ONLINE

Go online to the Digital Zone and click the links to listen to *Die schöne Müllerin* and Schumann's *Fraunliebe und Leben* at www.brightredbooks.net/subjects.

11

MUSIC CONCEPTS
SONG CYCLE 2

Robert Schumann (1810–1856)

SCHUMANN'S *FRAUENLIEBE UND LEBEN* (*WOMAN'S LOVE AND LIFE*)

Schumann's *Frauenliebe und Leben* (*Woman's Love and Life*) is a cycle of eight songs based on poems by Adelbert von Chamisso. They tell the story of a young woman falling in love, becoming engaged, getting married, having a child, and finally mourning the death of her husband.

In the first song, *Seit ich ihn gesehen* (*Since mine eyes have seen him*), she sees the man of her dreams for the first time. The music is in the key of B flat major and has three beats in a bar. It starts gently with three chords on the piano before the mezzo-soprano voice enters. The song is in strophic form, each verse ending with an interrupted cadence.

ONLINE

Go online to the Digital Zone and click the link to listen to *Seit ich ihn gesehen* at www.brightredbooks.net/subjects.

ONLINE

Go online to the Digital Zone and click the link to listen to *Er, der Herrlichste von allen* at www.brightredbooks.net/subjects.

In the second song, *Er, der Herrlichste von allen* (*He, the best of all, the noblest*), she sings of the man's attractive qualities. The opening repeated chords on the piano suggest the woman's beating heart, before the voice enters with a phrase based on an arpeggio. The vocal line and piano part both feature **turns**. The overall form is rondo, with the piano interludes echoing the arpeggiated opening phrase.

contd

Music concepts: Song cycle 2

> **DON'T FORGET**
>
> A turn is an ornament consisting of four notes which turn around a main note, starting with the note above, followed by the main note, then the note below, and returning to the main note.

In the third song, *Ich kann's nicht fassen, nicht glauben* (*I cannot grasp or believe it*), we learn that the woman's love is reciprocated. The song is in a minor key, ending with a tierce de Picardie.

In the fourth song, *Der Ring* (*The Ring*), she gets engaged. The song is in ternary (ABA) form; section A has a flowing piano accompaniment, while section B features repeated chords played by the piano.

In the fifth song, *Helft mir, ihr Schwestern* (*Help me, sisters*), the woman is getting married. The arpeggios on the piano suggest the excited bustling of the bride being dressed by her sisters for the wedding ceremony. The song is in strophic form and the coda played on the piano suggests a wedding march.

In the sixth song, *Süsser Freund, du blickest* (*Sweet friend, you gaze*), the woman tells her husband she is going to have a baby. The song is in ternary (ABA) form with section A being like a recitative and section B featuring repeated chords on the piano.

In the seventh song, *An meinem Herzen, an meiner Brust* (*At my heart, at my breast*), she sings about her new baby. The structure of the song is strophic, with the accompaniment in the last verse changing from legato arpeggios to staccato chords. The slow piano coda suggests a mother gently rocking her baby.

> **ONLINE**
>
> Go online to the Digital Zone and click the link to listen to Schumann's *Frauenliebe und Leben* at www.brightredbooks.net/subjects.

In the eighth and final song, *Nun hast du mir den ersten Schmerz gethan* (*Now you have caused me pain for the first time*), the woman mourns the death of her husband. The music starts in a minor key and is like a recitative. The song ends with an extended piano solo in a major key, based on the music of the first song, reminding us of the joy of her initial love.

 THINGS TO DO AND THINK ABOUT

Listen to different songs from Schumann's *Frauenliebe und Leben*. In each case:

- identify the structure of the song (e.g. binary, ternary, strophic or through-composed)
- consider how the piano part contributes to the overall mood and character of the song
- identify any other prominent melodic, harmonic or rhythmic concepts in the music.

13

MUSIC CONCEPTS
SACRED MUSIC – MASS

HISTORICAL BACKGROUND

Composers throughout history have composed sacred music, which is music based on religious subjects, religious texts, or stories from the bible. In some cases, the music was composed specifically to be used for church services. In other cases, religious subjects have been used as the basis for choral works intended to be performed in a concert hall.

Musical styles associated with sacred music include plainchant, mass, motet, oratorio, anthem and chorale, some of which will already have learned about for Higher Music. Here you will explore more styles of sacred music from different periods in musical history. As you listen, you should consider which musical features place the music within a particular style or period.

DON'T FORGET

You will find examples and explanations of plainchant, mass and oratorio in the Bright Red Higher Music Study Guide.

SACRED MUSIC OF THE RENAISSANCE

During the Renaissance period (approximately 1450–1600) there was an increasing enthusiasm for learning and culture, with many important developments in artistic areas such as architecture, painting and music. Composers moved away from the limitations of Medieval plainchant, with its single-line melodies, exploring harmony and different musical textures. They started to blend musical strands together using either a simple homophonic (chordal) texture, or more complex polyphonic (contrapuntal) textures in which several strands of music would be weaved together in a continuous musical flow.

Some of the most important developments in music are to be found in the sacred choral music of the Renaissance, which would generally have been sung a cappella. The Italian term 'a cappella' literally means 'in the chapel style', suggesting that the music would be sung in a small church or chapel without instrumental accompaniment. Much of the music was also composed for four or more voice parts. However, as the convention of the time was for sacred music to be performed by male voices only, four-part choral works would generally feature trebles (boys' voices) singing the highest part rather than female sopranos, and high male voices singing the alto part, along with tenors and basses. Two of the most important styles of sacred music during the Renaissance were the **mass** and the **motet**, both of which were based on sacred Latin words.

DON'T FORGET

A mass is based on specific Latin texts: *Kyrie, Gloria, Credo, Sanctus* (*Osanna* and *Benedictus*), and *Agnus Dei*.

Latin headings of the five main sections of the mass, with English translations.

Latin	English
Kyrie eleison, Christe eleison	Lord have mercy, Christ have mercy
Gloria in excelcis Deo	Glory to God in the highest
Credo in unum deum	I believe in one God
Sanctus; Osanna; Benedictus	Holy, holy, holy; Hosanna; Blessed is he…
Agnus Dei	Lamb of God

MASS

Mass is the most important service in many Christian religions, including the Roman Catholic and Anglican churches. A typical mass is divided into five main sections, using specific Latin texts: *Kyrie, Gloria, Credo, Sanctus* (sometimes divided into *Sanctus, Osanna* and *Benedictus*), and *Agnus Dei*. It is also common for the *Gloria* and *Credo* to be introduced with a phrase of plainchant sung by a solo voice.

There are also other kinds of mass, e.g. *Missa Brevis* (a short mass) or *Requiem* (a mass for the dead), which may also include different texts.

Latin	English
Requiem æternam dona eis, Domine	Eternal rest give unto them, O Lord
Dies irae	Day of wrath
Lux æterna luceat eis	May light eternal shine upon them
Pie Jesu Domine	Gentle Lord Jesus
Libera me	Deliver me
In paradisum deducant te Angeli	May the Angels lead thee into paradise

Music concepts: Sacred Music – Mass

KYRIE AND GLORIA

The *Kyrie* and *Gloria* from the *Missa Brevis* by Palestrina illustrate some important musical features of Renaissance choral music. There are some notable musical similarities between the two movements – they are both composed for four voice-parts (trebles, altos, tenors and basses), performed a cappella, and in the same key. Each movement also features a suspension in the second last bar and ends with a perfect cadence.

The printed music of the *Kyrie* is in the key of F major. The music features four voice-parts (trebles, altos, tenors and basses), with boys singing the treble part and high male voices singing the alto part. It is performed a cappella. The mood is calm and serene, and the individual vocal lines are woven together to create a flowing and seamless polyphonic (contrapuntal) texture. The opening phrase forms the basis of the music; starting with the altos, imitated two bars later by the basses, then two bars after that by the trebles, and finally two bars later by the tenors. There is frequent use of imitation, with the voice entries overlapping one another as the music continues. Much of the word setting is melismatic.

The music also includes suspensions, where a note from one chord is held over to the next chord. A clear example of this is in the second last bar where the second note in the treble part (F) is held over to the next chord, resolving onto the third note (E). The music finishes with a perfect cadence.

The *Gloria* contains a number of similarities, but also some notable differences. It opens with a solo tenor voice singing a phrase of plainchant.

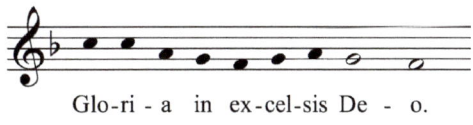

This is followed by the trebles, altos, tenors and basses all singing together. The texture here is homophonic (chordal) and the word setting is mainly syllabic.

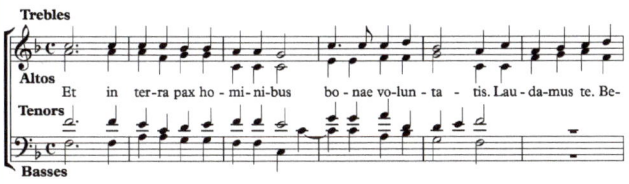

As the music continues, there is a mixture of polyphonic and homophonic textures. There are also more suspensions.

THINGS TO DO AND THINK ABOUT

Listen to other movements from masses by different composers so that you become more familiar with the various Latin texts of the mass. There are examples of masses from different styles and periods in the Bright Red Higher Music Study Guide.

ONLINE
You can listen to the *Kyrie* by clicking on the link at the Digital Zone www.brightredbooks.net/subjects

DON'T FORGET
Polyphonic (contrapuntal) texture is when all the parts have independent melodic interest.

DON'T FORGET
Melismatic word setting is when several notes are sung to one syllable.

ONLINE
You can listen to the *Gloria* online on our Digital Zone at www.brightredbooks.net/subjects.

DON'T FORGET
Homophonic texture is when all the parts move in a similar rhythm at the same time.

DON'T FORGET
Syllabic word setting is when each syllable is given one note only.

ONLINE TEST
Take our quick online test on Sacred Music at the Digital Zone www.brightredbooks.net/subjects.

MUSIC CONCEPTS

SACRED MUSIC – MOTET

THE FEATURES OF A MOTET

Latin	English
Veni Sancte Spiritus	Come, Holy Spirit
Haec Dies	This is the day
Ave Maria	Hail Mary
Jubilate Deo	Be Joyful in the Lord
O quam gloriosam est regnum	O How Glorious is the Kingdom
Ave Verum Corpus	Hail, True Body
O Magnum Mysterium	O Great Mystery

Examples of Latin texts used for motets, with English translations.

The **motet** is a short sacred choral work, in a single movement with a Latin text, composed mainly for Catholic church services. During the Renaissance, motets would generally have been sung a cappella. However, some motets from later periods have instrumental, or even orchestral, accompaniment.

Renaissance Motets

Although a motet is shorter than a mass, the mood would still be generally calm and serene, and it would contain many of the same musical features.

ONLINE

You can listen to *Absalon, fili mi* and Byrd's *Ave Verum* by clicking the link on the Digital Zone www.brightredbooks.net/subjects.

ACTIVITY:

The motet *Absalon, fili mi* by Josquin des Prez is a rich setting of David's lament upon the death of his son, as told in the bible. The Latin title translates as "Absalon, my son".

The music is in a major key and is sung a cappella. The texture is polyphonic throughout, with the voice parts entering in imitation, creating a smooth seamless flow. It starts with the trebles, followed by the altos, then the tenors and finally the basses. There are also a number of suspensions.

Absalon, fili mi

The motet *Ave Verum* is a short communion hymn. This setting, by Byrd, is in a minor key and sung a cappella by a mixed choir of sopranos, altos, tenors and basses (SATB).

Although there is some rhythmic independence between the voices, the texture at the start is homophonic overall, as the four voice parts move mostly at the same time. Notice the tierce de Picardie at the end of the fourth bar and an imperfect cadence at the beginning of the eighth bar.

Ave Verum

As the music continues, there is a mixture of homophonic and polyphonic textures, with the use of imitation particularly when the word "miserere" is repeated. There are also a number of suspensions, most notably on the extended "Amen" at the end. The motet ends with a plagal cadence and a tierce de Picardie.

A Baroque Motet

While it was common for Renaissance masses and motets to be sung a cappella, during the Baroque period it was more common to have some kind of instrumental accompaniment.

The motet *Salve Regina* by Lully was composed for three soprano voices accompanied by basso continuo. The title translates as "Hail Queen" or "Hail Holy Queen", and refers to Mary, the mother of Jesus. The music starts with a bass line played by the basso continuo (cello and organ). The harmonies are then filled out by an instrument such as the organ or harpsichord.

Like many Renaissance motets, the voices enter one at a time using imitation to create a polyphonic texture, although the texture becomes more homophonic towards the end of this section. However, the instrumental accompaniment, featuring the basso continuo,

DON'T FORGET

A motet is a short sacred choral work with a latin text.

contd

Music concepts: Sacred music — Motet

is much more characteristic of Baroque music. Also, the way in which the vocal lines are sometimes embellished with ornaments is another Baroque characteristic. The tonality of the music is minor and this opening section ends with a perfect cadence and a tierce de Picardie.

A Classical Motet

This setting of the motet *Ave Verum,* by Mozart, was composed for SATB choir, strings and organ. The music is in the key of D major and the mood is very solemn. It begins with a short introduction of two bars, played by the strings. The SATB choir then enters. The texture is mainly homophonic. The melody is very graceful, with an expressive descending chromatic motif in the second bar of the soprano part. The phrases are clear-cut and evenly balanced, mainly eight bars long. The first eight-bar phrase ends with an imperfect cadence while the second eight-bar phrase ends with a modulation to the dominant key and a perfect cadence.

The music is homophonic overall, although there is some imitation on the words "esto nobis".

It draws to a close with a short coda played by the strings, ending with a perfect cadence.

A Romantic Motet

The motet *Locus iste* by Bruckner is sung a cappella by a mixed SATB choir. The first line of the Latin text translates as "This place was made by God" and is intended for the anniversary of the dedication of a church.

The music is in the key of C major, although there are several chromatic chords and modulations to different keys, making the music very expressive. The word setting is mainly syllabic. The overall structure is ternary (ABA) form with the outer sections being mainly homophonic while the middle section is more polyphonic. The music ends with a perfect cadence.

Twentieth century Motet

The motet *O Magnum Mysterium* by Morten Lauridsen was composed for a double SATB choir. The Latin title translates as "O great mystery" and tells the story of the birth of Jesus. The music is in the key of D major, although it uses many discords and suspensions.

While this setting features many musical characteristics of Renaissance music (such as a calm mood, a cappella choir, a mainly homophonic texture but with some contrapuntal elements, and suspensions), it also features some important differences. The double SATB choir provides a richer and fuller sound, and there are varying levels of dynamics and slight changes in tempo. Also, the frequent use of discords suggest this is twentieth century music.

 THINGS TO DO AND THINK ABOUT

Compare different settings of the same text by different composers, identifying some prominent concepts as well as noting some similarities and differences.

For example:
- *Ave Verum* by Byrd and Mozart
- *O Magnum Mysterium* by Victoria and Lauridsen

 ONLINE

You can listen to *Salve Regina* by clicking the link on the Digital Zone www.brightredbooks.net/subjects.

 **DON'T FORGET**

Although a motet is based on a Latin text, it would be a different text from the mass.

 ONLINE

You can listen to Mozart's *Ave Verum* by clicking the link on our Digital Zone www.brightredbooks.net/subjects.

 ONLINE TEST

Take our quick online test on Sacred Music at the Digital Zone www.brightredbooks.net/subjects.

 ONLINE

You can listen to *Locus iste* by clicking the link at the Digital Zone www.brightredbooks.net/subjects.

 ONLINE

You can listen to contrasting setting while following the score *O Magnum Mysterium* by clicking the link on our Digital Zone at www.brightredbooks.net/subjects.

MUSIC CONCEPTS

SACRED MUSIC – ANTHEM 1

As well as the Mass and motet, with Latin words, composed for Catholic church services all over Europe, there was an increasing trend towards composers from different countries using words from their own native language for sacred works. Notable examples were the **anthem** (an Anglican choral work with English words), and the **chorale** (a Lutheran hymn tune with German words).

ANTHEM

An **anthem** is a short sacred choral piece sung in English, and was really the English equivalent of the Latin motet. However, whereas a Latin motet would have been composed for Catholic church services, an English anthem would have been composed for Anglican or Protestant services.

There are two main types of anthem: a *full anthem* and a *verse anthem*. A *full anthem* was composed for full choir and was generally sung a cappella. The convention at the time was that the choir would consist of male voices only, sometimes with choirboys singing the treble part and high male voices singing the alto part. However, high adult male voices, such as a male alto or countertenor, would also sometimes sing the higher voice parts.

In a *verse anthem*, the verses would be sung by one or more soloists, usually accompanied by an organ or viols (early string instruments), alternating with sections of the music for full choir.

Renaissance anthems

Here is a brief analysis of two contrasting anthems, *If ye love me* and *Hear the voice and prayer*, by the English Renaissance composer Thomas Tallis, noting some important similarities and differences.

Thomas Tallis (c.1505–1585)

 **ACTIVITY:**

The anthem *If ye love me* is based on a text taken from the Gospel of John from the Bible.

It is composed for four voice parts, performed a cappella, and would originally have been sung by male voices only. The printed music is in the key of F major and the time signature is 4/4.

The texture at the start is homophonic, although there is some use of imitation from bars 5–10. The music is in two sections, making it binary (AB) form – although, as the second section is repeated, the overall form is strictly ABB. The second section starts with the voice parts entering one at a time, using imitation. However, the overall texture is mainly homophonic. Both sections finish with a suspension followed by a perfect cadence.

 ONLINE

Go online and click the link to listen to the anthem *If ye love me* at the Digital Zone at www.brightredbooks.net/subjects.

 DON'T FORGET

An anthem is a short sacred choral work with English words.

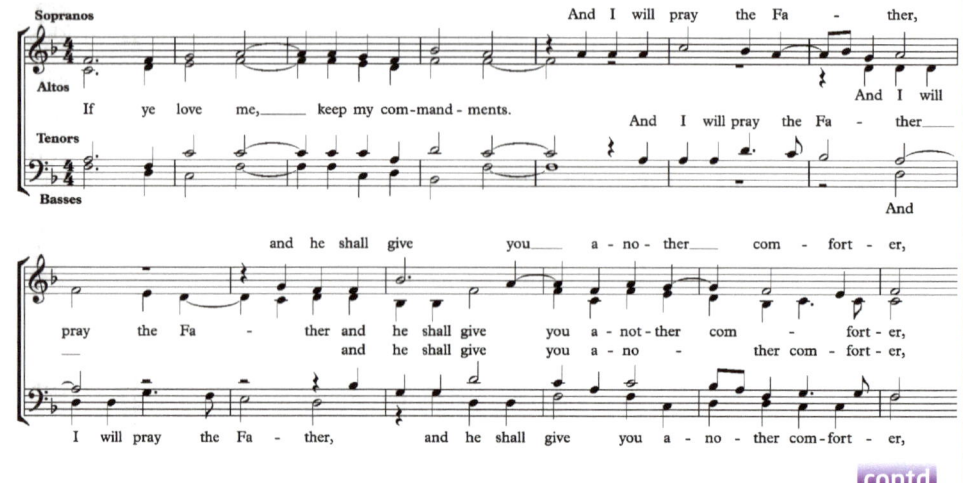

contd

Music concepts: Sacred music – anthem 1

The anthem *Hear the voice and prayer* is based on a passage from 1 Kings from the Bible.

This is also composed for four voice parts and performed a cappella. Again, it would originally have been sung by male voices only. The printed music is in the key of G minor and the time signature is 4/4. The music is structured in four phrases, with the first being the longest, and is in binary (AB) form overall.

The first section comprises the first phrase, while the second section comprises the second, third and fourth phrases. Therefore, as the second section (comprising phrases 2–4) is repeated, the overall structure may again be regarded as an extended binary form (ABB).

The texture at the beginning is polyphonic, with each voice part entering one after the other in imitation. Towards the end of this first section, at the words 'that they make before thee this day', the texture is homophonic. The section ends with a perfect cadence and a tierce de Picardie.

 ONLINE

Go online and click the link to listen to the anthem *Hear the voice and prayer* at the Digital Zone at www.brightredbooks.net/subjects.

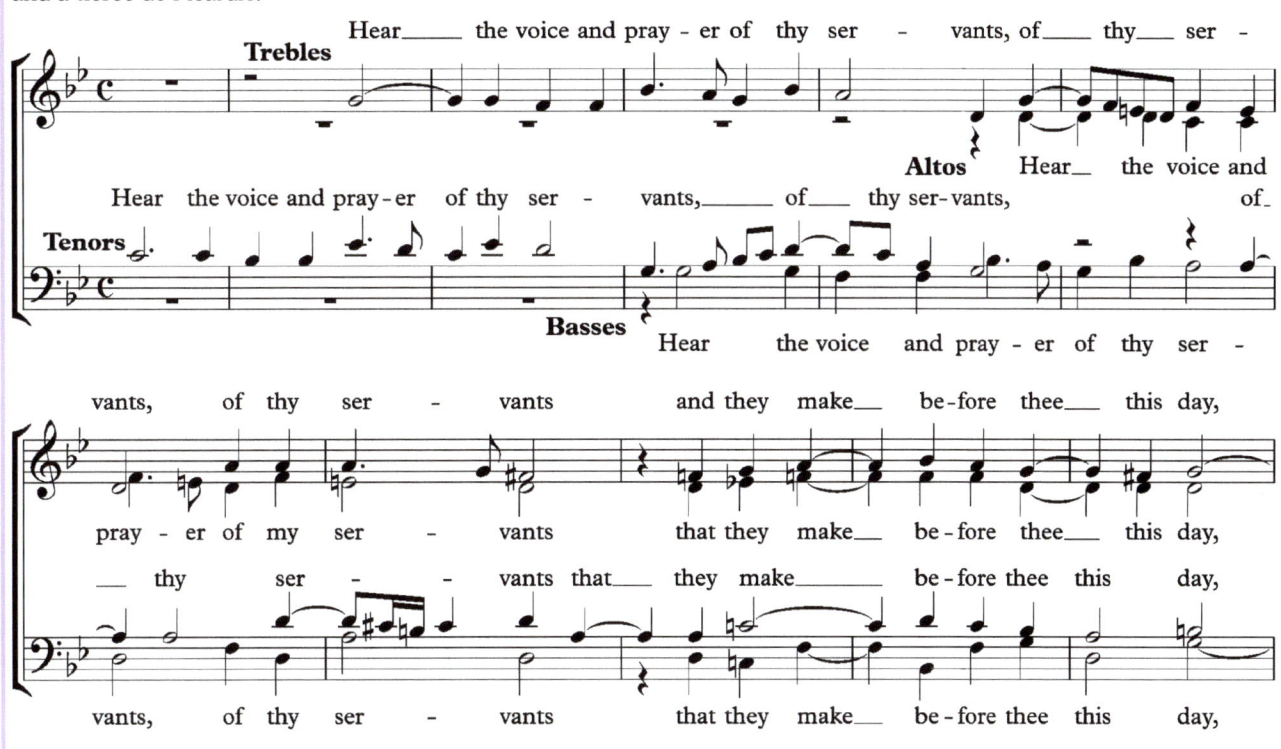

 THINGS TO DO AND THINK ABOUT

Listen to some other examples of anthems by composers from different musical periods. Try to identify some prominent concepts and consider which features place the music within a particular style or period.

Make a list of one or two prominent concepts under each the following headings:

- Style
- Melody/harmony
- Rhythm/tempo
- Texture/structure/form
- Timbre

 ONLINE

Go online and click the links to listen to examples of other anthems by composers from different musical periods at www.brightredbooks.net/subjects.

MUSIC CONCEPTS

SACRED MUSIC – ANTHEM 2

BAROQUE ANTHEMS

Whereas it was common throughout the Renaissance for anthems to be sung a cappella, during the Baroque period it was more usual to have some kind of instrumental accompaniment.

Henry Purcell

Rejoice in the Lord alway, also known as the 'Bell Anthem', by Purcell is composed for alto, tenor and bass soloists, four-part SATB choir, strings and continuo.

The music begins with an extended introduction for strings and organ. It is in 4/4 time and in the key of C major. A prominent feature of the introduction is the use of a ground bass comprising of a repeated descending C major scale. This is used to represent the peal of church bells, giving the piece its nickname the 'Bell Anthem'.

Henry Purcell (1659–1695)

ONLINE

Go online to the Digital Zone and click the link to hear this anthem by Purcell at www.brightredbooks.net/subjects.

After the introduction, the trio of soloists (alto, tenor and bass) enter, accompanied by the strings, with a much quicker section and a change in metre to 3/4 time. This section begins with an anacrusis and also features a number of dotted rhythms. The texture overall is homophonic. The music is still in the key of C major. However, there are some chromatic notes such as the F sharp (F#) in the tenor part at bar 5, suggesting a brief modulation to the dominant key of G major at bar 6. The section ends with a perfect cadence in the key of C major.

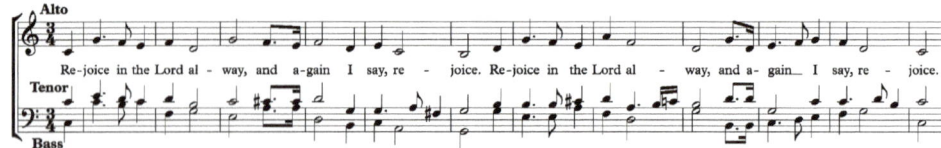

This music is echoed by the strings in the form of a ritornello, before the trio of soloists return, extending the text slightly with the use of imitation. The full SATB choir then enters, echoing and extending the music of the soloists, followed by the ritornello on the strings. We then hear the bass solo leading to a short passage with the other soloists in imitation: the bass followed by the tenor and then the alto. The texture quickly becomes homophonic again and there is another change of time signature from three to four beats in the bar. This is also echoed by the strings. Finally, there is a change back to 3/4 time with the soloists, followed by a short ritornello on the strings, and then the full SATB choir echoing the music of the first section. The music finishes with a perfect cadence.

George Frederic Handel

The anthem *Zadok the Priest* by Handel was composed for the coronation of King George II in 1727, and has been performed at each British coronation ever since. The words are taken from the *King James Bible*. The music is composed for a large choir consisting of two sopranos, two altos, tenor and two basses. The choir is accompanied by a Baroque orchestra consisting of two oboes, two bassoons, three trumpets, timpani, strings and continuo.

The music is in the key of D major and is divided into clear-cut sections. It starts with an extended orchestral introduction in common (4/4) time. A prominent feature of the introduction is the use of a repeated ascending broken chord pattern.

George Frederic Handel (1685–1759)

contd

20

Music concepts: Sacred music – anthem 2

The full choir then enters fortissimo with a short first section that ends with an imperfect cadence. The texture is homophonic.

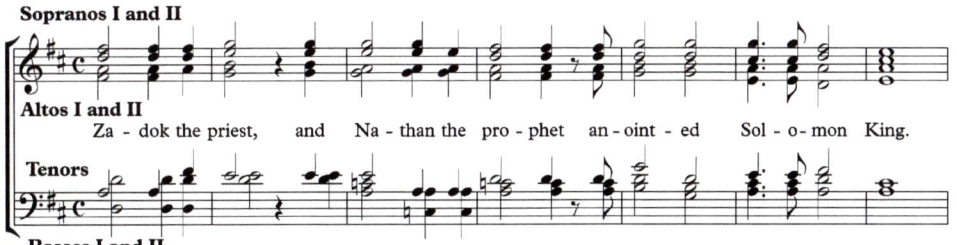

The second section is faster and changes to 3/4 time. The texture is homophonic and there are repeated perfect cadences on the word 'rejoiced'. A prominent feature of the accompaniment is the use of dotted rhythms, particularly in the brass and strings. The section ends slowly, with an imperfect cadence.

The third section returns to common (4/4) time. The texture overall is still homophonic, although a prominent feature of this section is the extended melismatic runs on the word 'Amen', taken in turn by the basses, sopranos, the altos and tenors together with the first basses, and finally the basses again. The music slows down at the end and draws to a close with a plagal cadence on the final 'Allelujah'.

THINGS TO DO AND THINK ABOUT

Listen to some other examples of anthems by composers from different musical periods. Try to identify some prominent concepts and consider which features place the music within a particular style or period.

Listen for the most prominent concepts and don't try to write down everything you hear.

Try to focus on features that are unique to a particular style or period.

ONLINE

Go online to the Digital Zone and click the link to hear *Zadok the Priest* by Handel at www.brightredbooks.net/subjects.

DON'T FORGET

Melismatic is a feature of vocal music where several notes are sung to one syllable

DON'T FORGET

An anthem is a short sacred choral work with English words.

ONLINE TEST

Test yourself on sacred music at www.brightredbooks.net/subjects

ONLINE

Go online and click the links to listen to examples of other anthems by composers from different musical periods at www.brightredbooks.net/subjects.

21

MUSIC CONCEPTS

SACRED MUSIC – CHORALE 1

Martin Luther (1483–1546)

ONLINE

Go online to the Digital Zone and click the links to see the original notation for this hymn and to listen to a version of it at www.brightredbooks.net/subjects.

CHORALE

A **chorale** is a type of hymn associated with the German Protestant church founded by Martin Luther in the early sixteenth century. As a result of a movement known as the Reformation, there was a move to encourage greater involvement of the congregation in singing during church services. A significant way in which this was achieved was through the introduction of singing hymns with German, rather than Latin, words. These hymns had short rhyming verses and the melodies had short, simple phrases that were easy to remember and therefore easy for the members of a congregation to sing.

The chorale tune *Ein feste Burg ist unser Gott* (*A mighty fortress is our God*), thought to have been composed by Martin Luther, displays many characteristics typical of the early Lutheran chorales.

The form of the verses is AAB, with section B being longer than section A. The overall structure of the chorale is strophic, as the same melody is repeated for each verse. The printed music is in the key of C major. This particular chorale is in 4/4 time and begins with an anacrusis, although the rhythm might be interpreted more freely. The early chorales would have been sung a cappella, and in unison.

Here is an English translation of the first verse:

> A mighty fortress is our God,
> A bulwark never failing:
> Our helper He, amid the flood
> Of mortal ills prevailing.
> For still our ancient foe
> Doth seek to work his woe;
> His craft and power are great,
> And armed with cruel hate,
> On earth is not his equal.

DON'T FORGET

A chorale is a German hymn tune often harmonised for SATB with a homophonic texture.

By the end of the sixteenth century, fewer new chorale tunes were being composed. However, in the course of the seventeenth century it became common practice for composers to arrange familiar chorale tunes in simple four-part harmony (for SATB) with the melody in the soprano voice for the congregation to sing along with. The other voice parts might have been either sung by a choir or provided as an instrumental accompaniment on the organ.

During the Baroque period, composers also incorporated SATB settings of chorale melodies into larger works such as oratorios, passions and cantatas. A passion is a type of oratorio based on biblical texts about the death of Christ, while a cantata is really a small-scale oratorio.

Music concepts: Sacred music – chorale 1

CHORALE SETTINGS BY BACH

The Baroque composer Johann Sebastian Bach is regarded as a significant figure in the development of the chorale. Although Bach did not actually compose any original chorale melodies, he is well known for harmonising chorale tunes of which there are over four hundred examples. Some of Bach's chorale settings are quite elaborate and many have very rich harmonies.

The chorale melody *O Haupt voll Blut und Wunden* (*O sacred head, now wounded*), originally composed by Hans Leo Hassler in around 1600, was famously harmonised by Bach. Also known as the *Passion Chorale*, it occurs five times in Bach's *St Matthew Passion*, each time in a different key and harmonised four different ways.

The form of the verses, like many chorales, is AAB, with section B being more extended. The music is divided into regular two-bar phrases, with a pause at the end of each phrase.

The overall structure of the chorale is strophic, as the same music is repeated for the two verses. This chorale is in common (4/4) time and begins with an anacrusis. The music is performed by a four-part SATB choir, accompanied by a Baroque orchestra doubling the voice parts, and the texture is homophonic.

An interesting feature of this particular chorale is that the music modulates several times. Section A starts in the key of F major and the first two-bar phrase ends with a perfect cadence in the tonic key. The second two-bar phrase modulates to the relative minor key. Section B returns to F major and the first phrase ends with a plagal cadence in the tonic key. The second phrase of section B modulates to a different minor key and ends with an imperfect cadence. The third phrase of section B then modulates to the dominant key, finishing with a perfect cadence in the key of C major. The fourth phrase returns to the tonic key of F major and ends with a perfect cadence.

Here is an English translation of the first verse:

> *O sacred Head, now wounded,*
> *with grief and shame weighed down,*
> *Now scornfully surrounded*
> *with thorns, Thine only crown;*
> *O sacred Head, what glory,*
> *what bliss till now was Thine!*
> *Yet, though despised and gory,*
> *I joy to call Thee mine.*

Johann Sebastian Bach (1685–1750)

ONLINE
Go online to the Digital Zone and click the links to see the original notation for the *Passion Chorale* and to listen to a version of it at www.brightredbooks.net/subjects.

ONLINE
Go online to the Digital Zone and click the links to listen to examples of other chorales by different composers at www.brightredbooks.net/subjects.

ONLINE TEST
To take an online test on this topic, go to the Digital Zone at www.brightredbooks.net/subjects

 ## THINGS TO DO AND THINK ABOUT

Listen to some other examples of chorales by different composers. Try to identify some prominent concepts and consider which features place the music within a particular style or period.

MUSIC CONCEPTS

SACRED MUSIC – CHORALE 2

MORE CHORALE SETTINGS BY BACH

The chorale *Wachet auf, ruft uns die Stimme* (*Awake, the voice is calling us*) was originally composed as a Lutheran hymn by Philipp Nicolai in the late sixteenth century. However, the melody has been used as the basis of many choral works and organ pieces since, including a chorale cantata of the same name by Bach.

Bach's cantata, just like an oratorio, features solo voices (soprano, tenor and bass), SATB chorus, and orchestra. The three verses of the chorale are set in different ways throughout the cantata. It is the third verse, however, that is typical of many chorales harmonised for SATB chorus.

The music is in a major key and in common (4/4) time. The overall structure, like many chorales, is AAB. Section A is divided into three phrases, with a pause at the end of each phrase. The first phrase modulates to the dominant key, ending with a perfect cadence. The second phrase remains in the dominant key, also ending with a perfect cadence. Both of these cadences also feature suspensions. The third phrase returns to the tonic key, again ending with a perfect cadence. While there is generally more movement in the bass part than the other parts, the texture is homophonic overall.

Here is an English translation of the text in section A:

> *May Gloria be sung to you*
> *with the tongues of men and angels,*
> *with harps and with cymbals.*
> *The gates are made of twelve pearls,*
> *in your city we are companions*
> *of the angels on high around your throne.*

Section B is divided into six short phrases, each ending with a pause. The first phrase, in the tonic key, ends with an interrupted cadence, while the second phrase ends with a suspension followed by a perfect cadence in the tonic key. The third phrase remains in the tonic key. The fourth phrase, which is very short, modulates to the relative minor key. The fifth phrase returns to the tonic key but ends with an interrupted cadence. The final phrase ends with a perfect cadence in the tonic key.

contd

ONLINE

Go online to the Digital Zone and click the link to listen to a version of Bach's chorale at www.brightredbooks.net/subjects.

DON'T FORGET

A suspension is a harmonic feature when a note from one chord is held over to the next chord creating a discord, which usually then resolves.

Music concepts: Sacred music – Chorale 2

Here is an English translation of the text in section B:

*No eye has ever perceived,
no ear has ever heard such joy.
Therefore we are joyful,
hurray, hurray!
for ever in sweet rejoicing.*

CHORALES IN OTHER CONTEXTS

The term 'chorale' can also be used in other contexts to describe any music that uses chorale-like features. For example, the final movement of the Symphony No. 2 by Gustav Mahler contains a short section for trombones, tuba and trumpets which is often described as a brass chorale due to its chorale-like phrase structure and homophonic texture.

The music is divided into clearly defined phrases, interspersed with short chromatic figures played pizzicato by the lower strings. The dynamic level gradually increases – starting pianissimo, then rising to piano, followed by a crescendo to forte and a further crescendo to fortissimo. At this point, there is a suspension and a dramatic snare drum roll before the full orchestra joins in with an even more dramatic section featuring strings, brass, timpani rolls, cymbal clashes and high trills on the woodwind.

🌧 THINGS TO DO AND THINK ABOUT

Listen to further examples of chorales by different composers. Again, try to identify some prominent concepts and consider which features place the music within a particular style or period.

➕ DON'T FORGET

A chorale is a German hymn tune often harmonised for SATB with a homophonic texture.

➡ ONLINE

Go online to the Digital Zone and click the link to the final movement of Mahler's Symphony No. 2 at www.brightredbooks.net/subjects.

✓ ONLINE TEST

To take an online test on this topic, go to the Digital Zone at www.brightredbooks.net/subjects.

➡ ONLINE

Go online to the Digital Zone and click the links to listen to further examples of chorales by different composers at www.brightredbooks.net/subjects.

25

MUSIC CONCEPTS

RENAISSANCE VOCAL MUSIC

Alongside developments in sacred music during the Renaissance, there were important developments in other styles of both vocal and instrumental music. Many non-religious songs were composed during the Renaissance, expressing a wide range of moods and emotions. They were performed in a variety of ways, sometimes by groups of singers or by a solo voice, either a cappella or with instrumental accompaniment. Different textures were also used, such as a polyphonic, homophonic or single-line melody with accompaniment. While different vocal styles emerged all over Europe, three styles developed particularly in England: the **madrigal**, the **ballett** and the **ayre** (or **air**).

DON'T FORGET

Through-composed is the structure of a song in which there is little or no repetition of the music for each verse.

ONLINE

Go online to the Digital Zone at www.brightredbooks.net/subjects and click the link to listen to *As Vesta was from Latmos Hill descending* and follow the full score of the music.

DON'T FORGET

A madrigal would generally be sung a cappella, have a polyphonic texture and be through-composed.

ONLINE TEST

To take an online test on this topic, go to the Digital Zone at www.brightredbooks.net/subjects.

MADRIGAL

The **madrigal**, also known as the *madrigal proper*, would have been composed for three to six voices, and sung a cappella. The individual voices would each have an interesting vocal line, and the texture would often be polyphonic with much use of imitation. The overall structure would be through-composed, although there is often repetition of the words themselves. Another common element of the madrigal is the use of *word-painting* – a technique by which composers would use specific musical features to vividly express the meaning or emotions of the words. For example, the word 'death' might be sung slowly to a harsh discord, while a phrase such as 'merry month' might be sung to a fast, joyful rhythm.

ACTIVITY:

As Vesta was from Latmos Hill descending by Thomas Weelkes was composed in honour of Queen Elizabeth I as part of a collection of English madrigals called 'The Triumphs of Oriana'. Elizabeth I was known as the 'maiden Queen' because she never married, and is referred to in the poem as Oriana.

The music is sung a cappella by six solo voices: two sopranos, one alto, two tenors and one bass. There is a rhythmic feel of two beats in the bar and the tonality is major overall. The texture is mainly polyphonic and the structure is through-composed. The music is also melismatic and contains many examples of word-painting.

The table offers an analysis of the song, indicating where a number of prominent musical features appear at particular words.

Text	Musical feature
As Vesta was from Latmos Hill descending,	Repetition and descending scales on 'descending'
She spied a maiden Queen the same ascending.	Ascending scales on 'ascending'
Attended on by all the shepherd's swain,	Repetition of words and use of suspensions
To whom Diana's darlings,	Imitation
Came running down amain.	Repetition of words, descending phrases and imitation
First two by two,	Two voices
then three by three	Three voices
together,	All voices singing
Leaving their Goddess all alone, hasted thither	Homophonic texture followed by a solo voice on 'all alone'
And mingling with the shepherds of her train,	Homophonic texture
With mirthful tunes, her presence entertain,	Polyphonic texture and use of imitation, followed by a suspension and a perfect cadence
Then sang the shepherds and nymphs of Diana	Homophonic texture
Long live fair Oriana!	Repeated phrases using imitation Ending with a suspension and a perfect cadence

26

Music concepts: Renaissance vocal music

BALLETT

The **ballett** is lighter in character than the madrigal and has clear-cut, dance-like rhythms. The texture is generally homophonic and the overall structure would be strophic. A noticeable feature of the ballett is the use of a recurring 'fa-la-la' refrain.

Sing we and chant it by Thomas Morley is a lively and joyful ballett composed for five voices: two sopranos, alto, tenor and bass. There is a lively rhythmic feel of three beats in the bar and the printed music is in the key of G major. The music is performed a cappella and the texture is mainly homophonic. There are two verses, both in binary form as they have two clear sections. However, as the same music is repeated for each verse the overall structure is strophic. Very typical of ballets, there is a recurring 'fa-la-la' refrain at the end of each section.

AYRE

The **ayre** (or **air**) is a song that could be performed in a variety of different ways: by a solo voice or by voices singing in harmony, either a cappella or with instrumental accompaniment.

Flow my tears by John Dowland is an expressive and melancholy ayre. The song is performed by a countertenor accompanied by a lute (a plucked string instrument played in a similar way to the guitar). The printed music is in the key of A minor and it has four beats in a bar. The texture is basically melody and accompaniment, although there are some contrapuntal elements in the accompaniment. The word-setting is mainly syllabic, and a number of suspensions are also featured.

The song is divided into three sections. The first section, in the key of A minor, has two verses ending with a perfect cadence and a tierce de Picardie. The second section, which also has two verses, starts in the relative major key of C major and ends with an imperfect cadence in the key of A minor. The third section has one verse which is repeated, and ends with a perfect cadence and a tierce de Picardie. While there is repetition within each of the three sections, the overall structure may still be regarded as through-composed.

THINGS TO DO AND THINK ABOUT

Listen to other examples of Renaissance vocal music, and consider the following questions.
- Is the music an example of a madrigal, a ballett or an ayre?
- What is the overall structure of the music (e.g. strophic or through-composed)?
- Is the music performed by a solo voice or a number of voices?
- Is the music performed a cappella, or is there any instrumental accompaniment?
- Is the texture homophonic, polyphonic or melody and accompaniment?

 DON'T FORGET

Strophic is the structure of a song in which the same music is repeated for each verse.

 **ONLINE**

Go online to the Digital Zone at www.brightredbooks.net/subjects and click the link to listen to *Sing we and chant it*.

 DON'T FORGET

A ballett would generally have a homophonic texture, be in strophic form, and have a recurring 'fa-la-la' refrain.

 DON'T FORGET

A countertenor is a very high male voice whose vocal range is similar to that of a female alto or mezzo-soprano.

 ONLINE

Go online to the Digital Zone and click the link to listen to *Flow my tears* at www.brightredbooks.net/subjects.

 DON'T FORGET

An ayre (or air) is generally a song for solo voice with instrumental accompaniment.

 ONLINE

Go online to the Digital Zone and click the links to listen to different examples of Renaissance vocal music at www.brightredbooks.net/subjects.

27

MUSIC CONCEPTS

RENAISSANCE INSTRUMENTAL AND DANCE MUSIC

Alongside developments in Renaissance vocal music, there were important developments in instrumental and dance music. Of the many types of dances composed during the Renaissance, two of the most popular were the **pavan** and the **galliard**. It was common for Renaissance dances to be performed by an instrumental ensemble called a **consort**.

Recorders

CONSORT

Consort is the term used to describe a small instrumental ensemble playing Renaissance music. Strictly speaking, the term *whole consort* is used to describe a group in which all the instruments come from the one family (e.g. strings or wind), whereas the term *broken consort* is used to describe a group in which the instruments come from more than one family (e.g. a combination of strings and wind).

PAVAN AND GALLIARD

The **pavan** and **galliard** were often performed as a pair of dances, with the galliard following the pavan. Each dance has its own individual character and distinct musical features, although the galliard is often based on a variant of the pavan tune. The pavan generally has a slow to moderate tempo, with a feeling of either two or four beats in a bar. It often has three sections and follows the form AABBCC.

The galliard is a quicker, sometimes lively, dance with three beats in a bar. Common rhythmic features of the galliard include the use of dotted crotchet-quaver-crotchet (♩.♪♩) rhythm and the use of **hemiola**. Renaissance dances often had some percussion accompaniment provided by a tambourine, a tabor (a large double-headed drum) or a tambour (a small hand-held drum, similar to a tambourine but without the jingles).

 ACTIVITY:

Typical features of the pavan and galliard can be found in the *Pavan and Galliard d'Angleterre* by the French Renaissance composer Claude Gervaise.

One of the performances features both a descant and a treble recorder playing the melody. A chordal accompaniment is provided by an early keyboard instrument called a spinet (a small type of harpsichord popular during the Renaissance). There is also a steady rhythmic accompaniment provided by a tambourine. The other performance is played by a consort of viols (an early type of bowed string instrument popular in the Renaissance), without any percussion accompaniment. The music was originally composed for a five-part instrumental ensemble with a homophonic texture.

Notice that both dances are based on the same melody, even though they have different time signatures. There are a number of other similarities. Both dances follow the same structure, having three clear sections, each of which is repeated. The first two sections are each four bars long, while the third section is eight bars long. Following the printed music, section A is in the key of F major and ends with a perfect cadence in the tonic key. Section B modulates to the relative minor and ends with a perfect cadence in the key of D minor. Section C starts in the tonic key of F major, but also ends with a perfect cadence in the key of D minor. The pavan is immediately followed by the galliard.

The differences are in tempo and rhythm. The pavan is played at a moderate tempo and has four beats in the bar. The galliard is quicker, has three beats in the bar, and features the characteristic dotted rhythm (♩.♪♩) in the second bar of section A and the second bar of section B.

ONLINE

Listen to contrasting performances of *Pavan and Galliard d'Angleterre* by clicking the link on the Digital Zone at www.brightredbooks.net/subjects. You will hear two contrasting performances of these dances, allowing you to gain an understanding of the musical features of each dance, as well as becoming familiar with different types of instrumental consorts.

DON'T FORGET

A pavan is generally a slow dance with two or four beats in the bar. A galliard is a quicker dance with three beats in the bar.

contd

Music concepts: Renaissance instrumental and dance music

Pavan

The *Pavan* from *Mr Allerton's Booke of Musick* is performed by a consort of recorders. The printed music of the main theme is in the key of G major, and there are four beats in the bar. The second bar ends with a plagal cadence, while the fourth, sixth and eighth bars all end with an imperfect cadence. The whole piece is based on this opening theme, which is first played by a descant recorder and then repeated by a bass recorder. While the theme is repeated again by the bass recorder, the descant recorder plays a countermelody featuring a combination of dotted and syncopated rhythms. The solo tenor recorder then begins a variant of this theme, with the other recorders joining in one at a time in imitation. The melody is finally played by the descant recorder again, followed by a very short coda ending with a perfect cadence.

Galliard

Although many Renaissance dances would have been performed by a consort, it would not have been uncommon for dances to be performed by a solo instrument such as a harpsichord or a lute.

The *Frog Galliard* by John Dowland is an example of a galliard that is often played on a lute or a guitar. The music is in the key of G major, has three beats in the bar, and features a number of dotted rhythms. Towards the end of this opening section there is also an example of a hemiola, where the notes in the lower part, with a tie across the bar, temporarily create a rhythmic feel of the music being in twos rather than threes.

As the music continues, the melodic line becomes more elaborate, with a number of semiquavers and triplets. The hemiola occurs at the end of each section.

THINGS TO DO AND THINK ABOUT

Listen to other examples of Renaissance dances, and consider the following questions.

- Is the music an example of a pavan or a galliard?
- Is the music performed by a consort or a solo instrument?
- If the music is performed by a consort, which instruments (or types of instrument) are playing?
- What rhythmic features are present in the music?

 ONLINE

Listen to the *Pavan* from *Mr Allerton's Booke of Musick* by clicking the link on the Digital Zone at www.brightredbooks.net/subjects.

 **DON'T FORGET**

Hemiola is a rhythmic device giving the impression of the pulse changing from triple (3) time to duple (2) time, or vice versa.

 ONLINE

Listen to the *Frog Galliard* by clicking the link on the Digital Zone at www.brightredbooks.net/subjects.

 ONLINE

Listen to different examples of Renaissance dances by clicking the link on the Digital Zone at www.brightredbooks.net/subjects.

 ONLINE TEST

To take an online test on this topic, go to the Digital Zone at www.brightredbooks.net/subjects.

MUSIC CONCEPTS
ANTIPHONAL TEXTURE

An **antiphonal** texture is when there is more than one group of instruments or voices, creating a kind of musical dialogue between the groups. A musical phrase from one group is answered by the same phrase, or a different phrase, from another group. The groups are usually placed apart to create a stereo or spatial effect.

St Mark's Cathedral, Venice

This contrasting effect was often used by Renaissance composers in St Mark's Cathedral in Venice. The cathedral has two organ lofts, set up high to the left and right of the organ. Each loft could hold singers and instrumentalists, and music would be composed so that the two groups would be well contrasted.

ACTIVITY:

The *Sonata Pian' e forte* by Giovanni Gabrieli explores contrasts between timbre, pitch and dynamics. The music is performed by two contrasting groups of brass instruments: one group consists of higher pitched instruments (two cornets and two French horns), while the other consists of lower pitched instruments (three trombones and tuba). Some performances use slightly different combinations of instruments while achieving the same overall effect. The two groups play sometimes separately and sometimes together. The title refers to the contrast in dynamics – this is the first instrumental piece to have dynamic marking to indicate contrast between piano (soft) and forte (loud).

The music has four beats in the bar and is modal. The structure is through-composed as there is no repetition of any section. The first section features the higher pitched brass instruments playing piano (softly). There is a mixture of polyphonic and homophonic textures, and also a number of suspensions.

ONLINE

Listen to *Sonata Pian' e forte* by clicking the link on the Digital Zone at www.brightredbooks.net/subjects.

DON'T FORGET

An antiphonal texture is when two or more groups of instruments or voices alternate to create a question-and-answer effect.

The second section features the lower pitched brass instruments and is also played piano. Again, there is a mixture of polyphonic and homophonic textures and a number of suspensions.

The two groups of instruments then play together. The dynamic level at this point is forte and the texture is polyphonic. As the music continues, the antiphonal texture becomes more prominent as there are more rapid question-and-answer effects between the two groups. The contrast between the piano and forte dynamic levels also becomes more prominent.

ONLINE

Listen to *O Magnum Mysterium* and *In Ecclesiis* by clicking the links on the Digital Zone at www.brightredbooks.net/subjects.

ACTIVITY:

Gabrieli also composed a number of motets featuring antiphonal textures. Listen to two contrasting motets such as *O Magnum Mysterium* and *In Ecclesiis* and identify some similarities and differences. As well as listening out for the antiphonal effects, consider the following questions.

- Does the music feature choirs, soloists or both?
- Is the music performed a cappella or with instrumental accompaniment?
- Are there any other prominent features in the music?

contd

Music concepts: Antiphonal texture

ANTIPHONAL TEXTURES IN OTHER STYLES OF MUSIC

Antiphonal textures have been used by many other composers from different styles and periods. The *Bourée* from *Music for the Royal Fireworks* by Handel is an example of antiphonal effects in a piece of Baroque music. The structure of the music is binary form.

Section A is played by two oboes and bassoon, and is repeated by two violins, cello, double bass and harpsichord continuo.

Section B is also played by two oboes and bassoon, and is repeated by two violins, cello, double bass and harpsichord continuo. The whole movement is then played again by all the instruments together, but without the repeats.

Fantasia on a Theme of Thomas Tallis by Vaughan Williams is a twentieth-century piece based on a tune by the Renaissance composer Thomas Tallis. The music is composed for two string orchestras (one large and one small) and a string quartet. The opening features a series of pianissimo chords played arco by all the strings. Two solo violins then play an inverted pedal, while a motif based on the opening of the original Tallis melody is played pizzicato by the lower strings. We then hear the complete theme, played arco by the second violins, violas and cellos. The melody is modal and there are a number of time changes.

This theme is then repeated by the first violins, an octave higher, while the second violins play a number of arpeggio and broken chord figures. As the music continues the instruments divide into contrasting groups and the texture becomes antiphonal. The large string orchestra often plays fortissimo (very loud), while the small orchestra plays pianissimo (very quiet). There are various antiphonal exchanges between the three groups, as well as solos from the viola and violin, before ending on a final fortissimo chord that fades away with a long diminuendo.

West Side Story is a classic musical by Leonard Bernstein and Stephen Sondheim, inspired by Shakespeare's play *Romeo and Juliet*. In one scene, members of the Puerto Rican gang (the 'sharks') argue with their girlfriends about life in America compared with life back home in Puerto Rico. The song *America* features a number of antiphonal exchanges between the boys and the girls, sometimes between solo voices and sometimes between the two groups. A prominent rhythmic feature of the song is the use of time changes. The music frequently alternates between 6/8 time and 3/4 time.

THINGS TO DO AND THINK ABOUT

Listen out for antiphonal effects in other songs from musicals, such as *Summer Nights* from *Grease* and *At the End of the Day* from *Les Misérables*, as well as some other popular songs.

ONLINE
Listen to *Bourée* by clicking the link on the Digital Zone at www.brightredbooks.net/subjects.

ONLINE
Listen to *Fantasia on a Theme of Thomas Tallis* while following the score by clicking the link on the Digital Zone at www.brightredbooks.net/subjects.

DON'T FORGET
Time changes involve a change in time signature – such as from three beats in a bar to four beats in a bar, or from simple time to compound time.

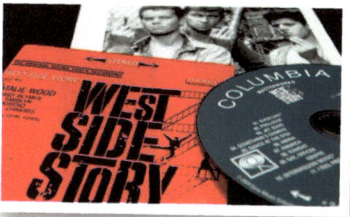

ONLINE
Listen to *America* from *West Side Story* by clicking the link on the Digital Zone at www.brightredbooks.net/subjects.

ONLINE
Listen to *Summer Nights* and *At the End of the Day*, and some other examples of songs that use antiphonal effects, by clicking the links on the Digital Zone at www.brightredbooks.net/subjects.

MUSIC CONCEPTS
FUGUE

A **fugue** is a contrapuntal (or polyphonic) composition based mainly on imitation. The texture is made up of separate strands of melody (usually three or four) called *parts* or *voices*, which are commonly referred to as soprano, alto, tenor and bass, whether the fugue is instrumental or vocal.

A fugue is generally structured in three main sections, called *exposition*, *middle section* and *final section*. However, these sections are not always clearly defined and often overlap. A complete fugue would usually be based on a single melodic idea called the *subject*. In the exposition, the subject would first be heard in one voice only and then imitated by the other voices in turn. This first statement of the subject is in the tonic key. A second voice then imitates the opening subject, usually in the dominant key. This imitation of the subject is called the *answer*. A third voice then enters with another statement of the subject in the tonic key and, sometimes, a fourth voice follows with another statement of the answer. Once the subject and answer have been heard in each voice, this is known as the exposition.

After a voice has stated the subject or the answer, it continues with a new contrapuntal melody. If each voice continues with the same melodic idea, this is called the **countersubject**. However, sometimes a voice might continue with a different melodic idea that does not recur regularly. This is called a *free part*, which might feature completely new ideas, although it can also use some melodic fragments from either the subject or the countersubject.

DON'T FORGET

Inversion is when a melodic phrase is turned upside down, creating a mirror image of the original phrase.

Sometimes the answer starts before the subject has finished, especially as a fugue progresses. This is called **stretto**. Throughout the fugue the subject would be heard in a variety of different keys, interspersed with episodes, which are often based on melodic fragments taken from either the subject or the countersubject.

The table below outlines a typical exposition of a fugue for four voices.

Voice 1	Subject (tonic) ▲▲▲▲▲▲▲▲	Countersubject ●●●●●●●●●●●●	Free part ◊◊◊◊◊◊◊◊◊◊◊◊◊◊◊◊◊◊◊◊◊◊◊◊◊◊◊◊◊◊
Voice 2		Answer (dominant) ▲▲▲▲▲▲▲▲	Countersubject ●●●●●●●●●●●●	Free part ◊◊◊◊◊◊◊◊◊◊◊◊◊◊◊
Voice 3			Subject (tonic) ▲▲▲▲▲▲▲▲	Countersubject ●●●●●●●●●●●●
Voice 4				Answer (dominant) ▲▲▲▲▲▲▲▲

Other musical devices commonly used in fugues include pedal, inverted pedal augmentation, diminution and inversion. Sometimes a composer might not compose a complete fugue, but will use some of the musical features associated with fugue. In this case the term *fugal* is used to describe the music.

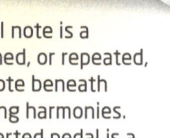

DON'T FORGET

A pedal note is a sustained, or repeated, bass note beneath changing harmonies. An inverted pedal is a high note which is held on, or repeated, over changing harmonies.

The Baroque composer J S Bach is regarded as one of the most influential figures in the development of the fugue. Bach composed many fugues, including a collection, *Forty-eight Preludes and Fugues*, consisting of two books – each containing twenty-four preludes and fugues, one in each of the twelve major and minor keys.

ACTIVITY:

Fugue No. VI from Book I is an example of a three-part fugue. In the exposition, voice 1 (soprano) introduces the subject in the key of D minor. Voice 2 (alto) then enters with the answer in the dominant key of A minor, while voice 1 continues with the countersubject. As voice 2 introduces the countersubject, and voice 1 continues with a free part based on some elements of both the subject and the countersubject, voice 3 (bass) enters with the subject in the tonic key. This completes the exposition. The music has three beats in the bar and both the subject and the answer feature a trill.

contd

32

Music concepts: Fugue

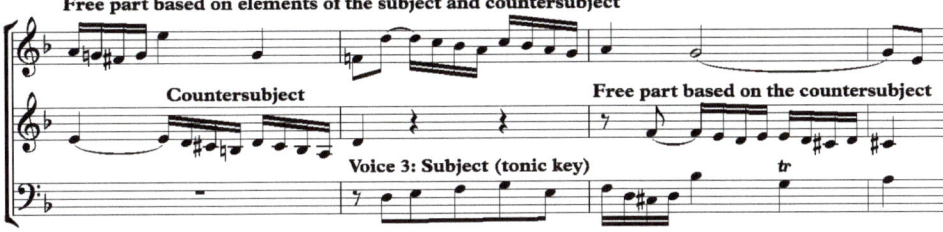

As the music continues there are also examples of inversion and stretto. The fugue finishes with both a pedal and an inverted pedal, with the final chord being a tierce de Picardie.

Fugue No. V from Book II is an example of a four-part fugue. In the exposition, voice 1 (tenor) introduces the subject in the key of D major. Voice 2 (alto) then enters with the answer in the dominant key. There is no countersubject here, so voice 1 continues with a free part based on melodic fragments from the subject. Voice 3 (soprano) then enters with the subject in the tonic key, quickly followed by voice 4 (bass) entering with the answer in the dominant key. This early entry of the answer in voice 4, before the subject has finished in voice 3, is an example of stretto.

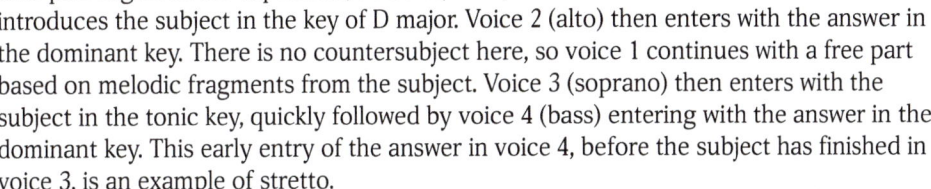

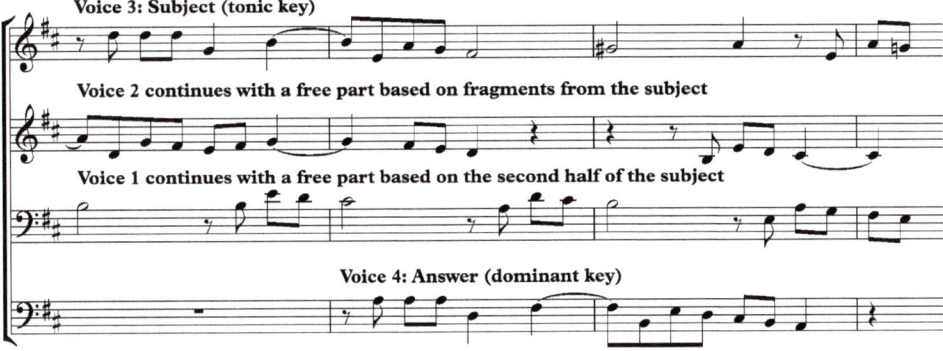

As the music continues there are several examples of stretto entries.

- At bars 14–15 there is the first example of a two-voice stretto, with the second voice entering half a bar after the first. Another example of this occurs at bars 23–24.

THINGS TO DO AND THINK ABOUT

Comparing two performances of the same fugue

Listen to two contrasting performances of Fugue No. II from Book I of Bach's *Forty-eight Preludes and Fugues* – one instrumental and one vocal. Compare the two performances, identifying some prominent concepts and noting any important similarities and differences.

DON'T FORGET

A tierce de Picardie is when a major chord is heard at the end of a piece of music in a minor key.

ONLINE

Listen to Bach's Fugue in D minor by clicking the link on the Digital Zone at www.brightredbooks.net/subjects.

DON'T FORGET

Stretto is part of a fugue where the answer starts before the subject has finished.

ONLINE

Listen to Bach's Fugue in D major by clicking the link on the Digital Zone at www.brightredbooks.net/subjects.

ONLINE

Listen to the two performances of Bach's Fugue No. II by clicking the link on the Digital Zone at www.brightredbooks.net/subjects.

ONLINE TEST

To take an online test on this topic, go to the Digital Zone at www.brightredbooks.net/subjects.

MUSIC CONCEPTS
CHORAL FUGUES

ONLINE

Listen to Handel's *He trusted in God* from *Messiah* by clicking the link on the Digital Zone at www.brightredbooks.net/subjects.

Many composers have incorporated fugues into choral works. *He trusted in God* from Handel's oratorio *Messiah* is an example of a fugue for four voices. It starts with a subject, sung by the basses in a minor key, which has four beats in the bar.

Basses: He trust-ed in God that He would de-li-ver Him: let Him de-li-ver Him, if he de-light in him.

The tenors then enter with the answer in the dominant key, followed by the subject sung by the altos in the tonic key, and then the answer sung by the sopranos in the dominant key. The music continues with a contrapuntal texture and prominent use of sequences. At the very end the music suddenly slows down, the texture becomes homophonic, and it draws to a close with three staccato chords, a suspension and a perfect cadence.

ONLINE

Listen to Mozart's *Kyrie* from the *Requiem Mass* by clicking the link on the Digital Zone at www.brightredbooks.net/subjects.

The *Kyrie* from Mozart's *Requiem Mass* is an example of a *double fugue* as it has two subjects. The first subject is introduced by the basses with the words 'Kyrie eleison', while the second subject is introduced by the sopranos with the words 'Christe eleison'. These two subjects always appear as a pair throughout the movement.

DON'T FORGET

A tritone is the interval of an augmented 4th, which is made up of three whole tones.

FUGUES IN DIFFERENT STYLES

The song *Cool* from the musical *West Side Story*, by Leonard Bernstein and Stephen Sondheim, contains several interesting musical features, including a fugue. The music begins with an instrumental introduction featuring time changes, syncopation and the prominent use of the **tritone**. The tritone also features prominently at the start of first two phrases of the vocal section.

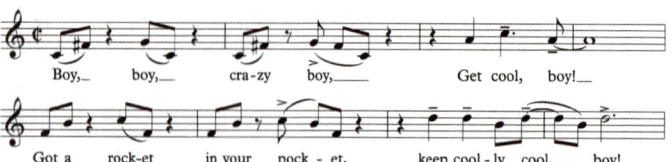

Boy, boy, cra-zy boy, Get cool, boy!
Got a rock-et in your pock-et, keep cool-ly cool, boy!

At the end of the second verse there is a short instrumental section based on the same musical ideas from the opening. This leads into a dance section, which is structured in the form of a fugue. An interesting feature of the fugue subject, which has three phrases, is that it is based on all twelve notes of the chromatic scale. Each of the three phrases uses four different notes.

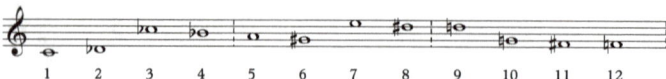

The full subject is played by muted (con sordino) trumpets, interspersed with short fragments played by the vibraphone and electic guitar. The first two phrases are both based on three long notes, with a short sforzando note at the end. The third phrase is based on shorter notes. The drum kit plays a swing rhythm throughout.

The countersubject has a more rhythmically complex and chromatic melody, in the style of a jazz improvisation, played by the flute and vibraphone.

ONLINE

Listen to *Cool* by clicking the link on the Digital Zone at www.brightredbooks.net/subjects.

Music concepts: Choral Fugues

As the fugue continues there are several sforzando chords. This is followed by a heavily syncopated melody played in unison and octaves, interspersed with drum kit solos. Then ideas from the introduction lead into a big band version of the melody from the song section, combined with elements of the countersubject from the fugue. After a return to the song for a final verse, there is a diminuendo featuring part of the countersubject, along with a swing rhythm on the drum kit and offbeat finger snaps.

The song *Fugue for Tinhorns* from the musical *Guys and Dolls*, by Frank Loesser, depicts three small-time gamblers arguing over which horse will win a big race. Strictly speaking, this is not a fugue as the second and third entries of the melody are both in the same key as the first entry. Therefore, it's more like an extended round or canon. However, the song does use features associated with fugue. After an introductory trumpet fanfare, the first voice enters with a solo over a vamping accompaniment. This could be regarded as a subject. The second voice then enters in imitation, while the first voice continues with what could be regarded as a countersubject. The third voice then enters very soon after the second, and so could be regarded as an example of stretto. The song continues with a contrapuntal texture and prominent use of imitation until the end, when the final phrase is homophonic.

ONLINE

Listen to *Fugue for Tinhorns* by clicking the link on the Digital Zone at www.brightredbooks.net/subjects.

 THINGS TO DO AND THINK ABOUT

Composing a fugue

Experiment with some techniques associated with fugue, and consider incorporating them into your own composition. The guide below takes you through a step-by-step approach to composing a simple exposition with three parts (or voices).

1. Create a short subject which could be harmonised easily. The example given is two bars long, in the key of C major, and uses just five notes.

   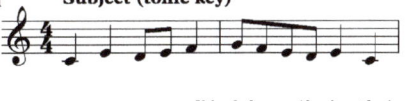

2. Create the answer by transposing the subject into a new key. In this example the subject is in the alto voice and is imitated in the dominant key (G major) by the soprano voice.

   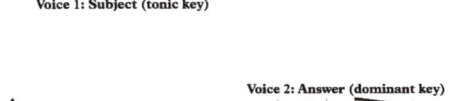

3. Create a countersubject in the alto voice that will fit along with the answer in the soprano voice. Using intervals such as 3rds and 6ths will help the harmony to sound full. Also, using some contrary motion will make the individual lines more interesting and independent.

4. Extend the answer in the soprano voice by adding the countersubject in the dominant key. In this example the countersubject has been amended slightly to ensure a smooth transition back to the tonic key.

5. Create a free part in the alto voice to fit along with the countersubject in the soprano voice. Again, using intervals such as 3rds and 6ths will help the harmony to sound full.

6. Introduce the final entry of the subject in the bass part.

7. Create two free parts for the soprano and alto voices, to fit above the subject in the bass. Putting this together gives you an example of an exposition of a fugue.

   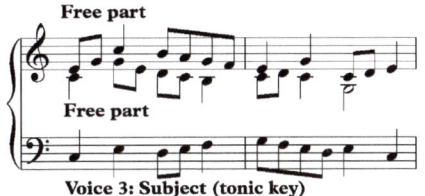

 **DON'T FORGET**

Adding some passing notes might also make the individual lines interesting.

 ONLINE TEST

To take an online test on this topic, go to the Digital Zone at www.brightredbooks.net/subjects.

MUSIC CONCEPTS
PIANO TRIO

A **piano trio** is a piece of music composed for three instruments – a piano and two other instruments. Most commonly the other instruments are a violin and a cello, but there are examples of trios composed for a piano and two different instruments.

CLASSICAL PIANO TRIO

The piano trio in the Classical period was often dominated by the piano part.

 **ACTIVITY:**

The third movement of the Piano Trio No. 25 by Haydn is a typical example of this. Nicknamed the 'Gypsy Rondo', because it is made up of lively and rhythmic Hungarian-style tunes, the piano plays the opening theme, which is immediately repeated by the violin an octave higher. This theme is in the key of G major, has two beats in the bar, and starts with an anacrusis.

The Trio in E flat major, K498 by Mozart is composed for piano, clarinet and viola. Mozart contrasts the individual timbres and playing techniques of the instruments, treating all three with equal importance. The first movement, 'Andante', is in sonata form. The first subject begins with a short phrase played by the piano and viola in unison, followed by an answering phrase on the piano. Another phrase is also played by the piano and viola in unison, again followed by an answering phrase played by the piano. The clarinet then plays a more extended phrase, along with a broken chord accompaniment on the piano. The piano takes up this melodic idea while the viola provides a broken chord accompaniment. A prominent feature of this first subject is the frequent use of turns.

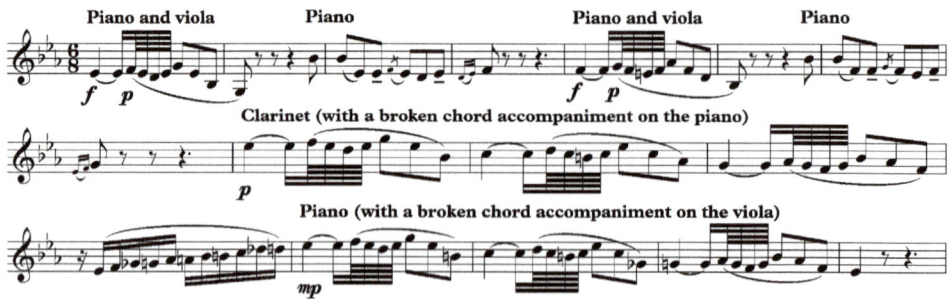

The Piano Trio in B flat major, Op. 97 by Beethoven is composed for piano, violin and cello. Beethoven gives all three instruments a high degree of independence. The music starts with a majestic theme played on the piano. The right hand plays the melody in octaves, while the left hand provides a repeated chordal accompaniment. This opening theme is then extended and varied, with elements being shared between all three instruments.

 ONLINE

Listen to Haydn's Piano Trio by clicking the link on the Digital Zone at www.brightredbooks.net/subjects.

 DON'T FORGET

A turn is an ornament consisting of four notes which turn around a main note, starting with the note above, followed by the main note, then the note below, and returning to the main note.

 ONLINE

Listen to Mozart's 'Andante' by clicking the link on the Digital Zone at www.brightredbooks.net/subjects.

 ONLINE

Listen to Beethoven's 'Archduke Trio' by clicking the link on the Digital Zone at www.brightredbooks.net/subjects.

Music concepts: Piano trio

ROMANTIC PIANO TRIO

The Piano Trio No. 1 by Mendelssohn, composed for piano, violin and cello, is typical of the Romantic style. The first movement is in sonata form, in the key of D minor, and has three beats in a bar. The opening theme is played by the cello, then taken up by the violin, while the piano creates tension by providing a syncopated chordal accompaniment. This is followed by some rapid arpeggios on the piano based on diminished 7th chords. The violin and cello then join in together, while the piano provides an accompaniment based on chromatic triplets in the right hand but with fragments of the opening melody played dramatically in the left hand using octaves. All three instruments then continue to interweave with a contrapuntal texture, before the cello introduces the second subject in the dominant major key.

DON'T FORGET

A diminished 7th chord is based on three intervals of a minor 3rd, built one on top of the other, the interval between the top and bottom note being a diminished 7th.

DON'T FORGET

Chamber music is music composed for a small group, generally intended to be performed in a palace chamber or large room rather than a large concert hall. Examples are sonatas, string quartets and piano trios.

A TWENTIETH-CENTURY PIANO TRIO

The Piano Trio by Ravel is composed for piano, violin and cello. Although the music is in the key of A minor, it has a distinct modal quality, which, along with the chromatic harmonies, suggests a twentieth-century Impressionist style. The music begins with the piano, quickly joined by the violin and cello playing the same melody two octaves apart. A prominent feature of this movement is the frequent use of an irregular rhythm pattern – while the time signature is 8/8, implying eight quavers in each bar, there is a rhythmic feel of 3 + 2 + 3, which is characteristic of folk music from the Basque region of southern France.

ONLINE

Listen to Mendelssohn's Piano Trio No. 1 by clicking the link on the Digital Zone at www.brightredbooks.net/subjects.

ONLINE

Listen to Ravel's Piano Trio by clicking the link on the Digital Zone at www.brightredbooks.net/subjects.

THINGS TO DO AND THINK ABOUT

Compare two examples of piano trios by different composers, noting some similarities and differences. Identify some prominent concepts in each and consider which features place the music within a particular style or period.

MUSIC CONCEPTS
LIETMOTIF

A **leitmotif** (*leitmotiv* or *leading motif*) is a recurring musical theme used to represent a person, place, emotion, object or idea. It could be a melodic phrase, a chord progression, or a rhythmic figure. The concept is associated with the operas of the Romantic composer Richard Wagner. However, the technique has also been used in orchestral pieces known as *symphonic poems* or *tone poems*, as well as in film music.

Wagner (1818–1883)

LEITMOTIF IN OPERA

Wagner composed a cycle of operas called *Der Ring des Nibelungen* (*The Ring of the Nibelung*). Known as 'The Ring', the cycle is made up of four separate operas intended to be performed over four consecutive evenings: *Das Rhinegold* (*The Rhinegold*), *Die Walküre* (*The Valkyrie*), *Siegfried* and *Götterdämmerung* (*The Twilight of the Gods*).

Rather than structuring the operas with individual recitatives, arias and choruses, Wagner used a technique that he called 'endless melody', in which the music flows continuously. This involved using leitmotifs – recurring themes which represent different elements in the story, for example characters (such as Siegfried and Brünnhilde), objects (such as the gold, the ring, and the sword), places (such as the river Rhine and Valhalla, home of the gods), and emotional elements (such as love, destiny and death). Some of the leitmotifs are very short, consisting of just a few notes, while others are more extended melodies.

ACTIVITY:

Here are some examples of leitmotifs from *The Ring*.

- *The gold*. Played by the trumpet, the fanfare-like motif begins with an anacrusis and is accompanied by the shimmering sound of strings and harps, with the percussion at the end suggesting the glittering of the gold.

- *Valhalla*, home of gods and heroes. Played gently by trombones and tubas with a homophonic texture, while a fanfare-like figure can be heard in the distance on the trumpet.

- *Donner, God of Thunder*. Heard first in the voice part, and echoed later by French horns, this motif is followed by a timpani roll, suggesting the sound of thunder.

- *The rainbow bridge*. The melody is played by the cellos and is based on an ascending and descending arpeggio figure, suggesting the arcing shape of a rainbow.

- *The sword*. Played on the trumpet, this motif starts with an anacrusis and features an octave leap followed by a rising arpeggio.

- *Love*. This leitmotif is a more extended theme. Played by a solo violin, a prominent feature of this expressive melody is the use of chromatic notes.

DON'T FORGET

A leitmotif is a recurring musical theme used to represent a person, place, emotion, object or idea.

ONLINE

Listen to the leitmotifs from *The Ring* and find out more about them by clicking the links on the Digital Zone at www.brightredbooks.net/subjects.

ONLINE

You will hear the first five of these leitmotifs in the final scene from *Das Rhinegold – Entry of the Gods into Valhalla*. Listen to *Entry of the Gods into Valhalla* by clicking the link on the Digital Zone at www.brightredbooks.net/subjects.

contd

- *Siegfried*, the hero of the cycle. The theme is in the key of D minor and is played by a French horn. The music is in compound time and starts with an anacrusis.

- *Siegfried's horn call*. This is the motif Siegfried plays on his horn at various points in the cycle to announce his arrival or express his joy. It is in the key of F major and in compound time.
- *Siegfried, the hero*. This is a majestic theme in a major key, with a homophonic texture, played by the brass.
- *Brünnhilde, Siegfried's wife*. Played by a clarinet and echoed by a bass clarinet, this is a short motif featuring the interval of a falling 7th at the end.

LEITMOTIF IN ORCHESTRAL MUSIC

Many composers have used leitmotifs in orchestral works known as *symphonic poems* or *tone poems*. These are pieces of music based on a non-musical idea such as a poem, story, painting or landscape. *Till Eulenspiegels lustige Streiche* (*Till Eulenspiegel's Merry Pranks*) by Richard Strauss tells the story of a medieval rogue known for playing practical jokes. The music uses several leitmotifs to suggest various elements of the story.

ACTIVITY:

The music opens with an introductory theme played by the violins, regarded as a music equivalent of 'once upon a time…'.

The most important theme in the piece represents the character Till, and is played twice by the French horn. A fragment of Till's theme is immediately played in turn by the oboes and clarinets, and then by bassoons and lower strings together.

After a crescendo from the orchestra, the clarinet plays a short motif suggesting Till mischievously plotting his next prank. The first six notes of this motif are taken from the opening theme.

LEITMOTIF IN FILM MUSIC

Leitmotifs are often used in film music to represent a character, create a mood or emphasise an emotion.

Consider how heroes such as James Bond, Superman, or Indiana Jones are represented in music. Think about how themes from films such as *Jaws*, *Pirates of the Caribbean*, or *The Great Escape* create a mood or atmosphere. And consider how emotions are emphasised in film themes such as *ET*, *Schindler's List* or *The Lord of the Rings*.

THINGS TO DO AND THINK ABOUT

Listen to some film themes and consider how leitmotifs are used to represent a character, create a mood or emphasise an emotion.

DON'T FORGET

Leitmotifs can be found in operas, orchestral works, and film music.

ONLINE

Listen to *Till Eulenspiegel* and find out more about the story by clicking the link on the Digital Zone at www.brightredbooks.net/subjects.

ONLINE TEST

To take an online test on this topic, go to the Digital Zone at www.brightredbooks.net/subjects.

ONLINE

Listen to these film-theme leitmotifs by clicking the links on the Digital Zone at www.brightredbooks.net/subjects.

ONLINE

Listen to other film themes by clicking the links on the Digital Zone at www.brightredbooks.net/subjects.

MUSIC STYLES

NATIONALIST MUSIC

The nineteenth-century Romantic period was a turbulent time in history, with many social upheavals across Europe. Several areas saw growing political movements in support of national liberation and self-determination. This had a significant influence on music, with many composers of the time wanting to break away from the Austro-German music tradition that had dominated the eighteenth-century Classical period in favour of a new style that would be more representative of their own land.

FEATURES OF NATIONALIST MUSIC

Nationalist music involves composers deliberately expressing elements associated with a particular country in their music. Three main ways in which composers achieve this are by:

- incorporating folk-song melodies or traditional tunes into their compositions
- composing melodies, rhythms and harmonies which contain musical features associated with folk music and dance rhythms
- using historical themes, legends and folklore as the inspiration for *programmatic* works and operas.

DON'T FORGET

Nationalist is term used to describe music which incorporates elements of folk music, or is based on legends or folklore, of a particular country.

ACTIVITY:

The first composer regarded as an important figure in Nationalist music was Glinka, whose two operas, *A Life for the Tsar* and *Ruslan and Ludmilla*, were based on Russian history and folk tales. The *Overture* to Glinka's *Ruslan and Ludmilla* exhibits Russian influences. Following an introduction featuring fortissimo chords played by the whole orchestra, and rapid scales on the strings, the flutes, violins and violas play a lively first subject. After the bridge passage which features imitation in the woodwind and sforzando chords played by the full orchestra, the violas, cellos and bassoon play the second subject, which is in the style of a Russian folk song.

ONLINE

Listen to the *Overture* from *Ruslan and Ludmilla* by clicking the link on the Digital Zone at www.brightredbooks.net/subjects.

Smetana composed an opera about Czech peasant life called *The Bartered Bride*, and a set of six *symphonic poems* called *Má vlast* (*My Country*) inspired by the Czech countryside, legends and history. The best known of these is *Vltava*, a musical depiction of the country's main river from its source until it reaches the city of Prague.

The music, in the key of E minor, starts with the flute playing a murmuring melody in compound time, suggesting the start of the river as a forest stream. This is accompanied by pizzicato chords on the violins.

ONLINE

Listen to the *Vltava* by clicking the link on the Digital Zone at www.brightredbooks.net/subjects.

contd

40

Music styles: Nationalist music

The music builds up with the lower strings taking up this opening figure, while the violins and oboe play a broader theme, starting with an anacrusis, suggesting the stream growing into a mighty river.

As the music continues there are references to folk music, before this theme returns in a majestic and triumphant major key.

Land of the Mountain and the Flood by Hamish MacCunn is an example of an orchestral work that depicts Scotland. The title, which refers to the rugged Scottish landscape, is taken from the text of a poem by the Scottish writer Sir Walter Scott.

The music is in sonata form and is built on two contrasting subjects, both of which exploit melodic and rhythmic features associated with Scottish music. The first subject, in a minor key, is played by the cellos and then repeated by the violins. While the notated music contains several rests, the effect created is that of dotted rhythms and Scotch snaps (shown by the bracket). This is followed by a bridge section that provides a link to the second subject.

The second subject, in the relative major key of D major, is played by the second violins, repeated an octave higher by the first violins, and then by the full orchestra. The opening pentatonic phrase, which has three beats in a bar, is suggestive of a Scottish folk song or ballad.

Bartók and Kodály collaborated to collect Hungarian folk tunes, which they both incorporated into their own music. Kodály composed a musical play called *Háry János*, based on the legendary adventures of a Hungarian soldier. The music is now best known in an orchestral suite of six pieces. The fifth movement, *Intermezzo*, includes a gypsy tune, which is characteristic of Hungarian folk music. The melody is in the key of D minor and played by the strings. It also features a number of dotted rhythms and Scotch snaps, as well as a Hungarian instrument called the cimbalon.

THINGS TO DO AND THINK ABOUT

Listen to other examples of Nationalist music such as *Finlandia* by Sibelius, *Slavonic Dance No. 8* by Dvořák, *Rapsodie España* by Chabrier, *Romanian Folk Dances* by Bartók and *Hoe-Down* from *Rodeo* by Copland. Consider which particular features contribute towards these pieces being regarded as Nationalist.

ONLINE

Listen to *Land of the Mountain and the Flood* by clicking the link on the Digital Zone at www.brightredbooks.net/subjects.

DON'T FORGET

A bridge is a section of music that links two themes or subjects, and also modulates to the key of the second subject.

ONLINE TEST

To take an online test on this topic, go to the Digital Zone at www.brightredbooks.net/subjects.

ONLINE

Listen to *Intermezzo* from *Háry János* by clicking the link on the Digital Zone at www.brightredbooks.net/subjects.

ONLINE

Listen to examples of Nationalist music by clicking the links on the Digital Zone at www.brightredbooks.net/subjects.

MUSIC STYLES
SERIAL MUSIC 1

A wide range of music styles emerged during the twentieth century. While some composers took quite a traditional approach to music, others were more experimental. You will already be familiar with some concepts associated with twentieth-century music from N5 and Higher. For Advanced Higher, the additional twentieth-century styles that you will need to be familiar with are **serial** music (including related concepts such as **tone row / note row**, **inversion** and **retrograde**) and **Neoclassical** music, as well as concepts such as **bitonality**, **polytonality** and **sprechgesang**.

DON'T FORGET

You can revise twentieth-century music concepts and styles from previous levels by referring to the *Bright Red National 5 Music Study Guide* and the *Bright Red Higher Music Study Guide*.

Serial music, sometimes called *twelve-note* or *twelve-tone* music, is a method of composing atonal music developed by Arnold Schönberg. The basic principle of serial music is that all twelve notes of the chromatic scale are treated equally, so that no single note is emphasised more than any other. When using chromatic notes, it is acceptable to use enharmonic equivalents to make sure that each note is only used once. For example, either E flat or D sharp can be used but not both.

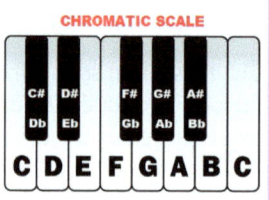
CHROMATIC SCALE

The composer arranges all twelve notes of the chromatic scale into a fixed order using each note once only. This is called the **note row** or **tone row**. The whole composition is then created using different permutations of this note row, sometimes in **retrograde** (reverse order), sometimes in **inversion** (upside down), and sometimes even in reverse order and upside down (*retrograde inversion*). The skill is in shaping the notes into melodies, constructing harmonies and textures, and creating rhythms, as well as choosing instrumental timbres.

DON'T FORGET

An enharmonic equivalent is when a note is called a different name but sounds the same. For example, B♭ (B flat) can also be called A# (A sharp).

In the *Variations for Orchestra,* Schönberg creates an extended theme using four permutations of a twelve-note row. Notice the variety of rhythms used to make the melody sound expressive and more interesting. Schönberg does occasionally repeat a note, though only when it's repeated immediately so as not to emphasise any one note too much. The first section of the theme is based on the *original* note row, using all twelve notes of the chromatic scale.

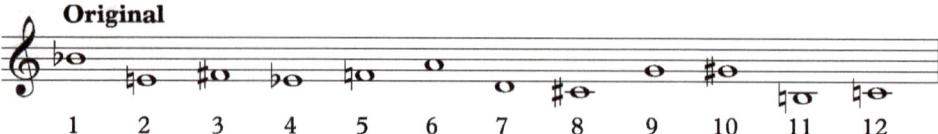

Notice how Schönberg has divided the note row into three short phrases, each starting with a rest.

Another section is based on the retrograde, using the same twelve notes, but in reverse order.

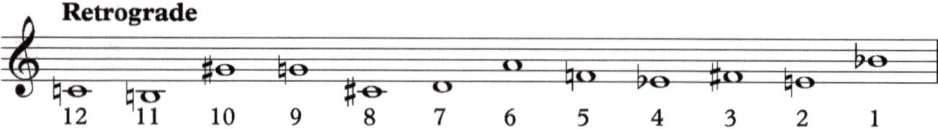

Schönberg has divided the retrograde version of the note row into two slightly longer phrases, each starting with a rest.

contd

42

Music styles: Serial music 1

The inversion shows a transposed version of the note row upside down, being a mirror image of the original.

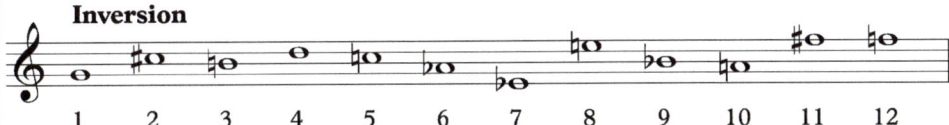

This version of the note row is divided into four short phrases, each starting with a rest.

Schönberg also uses a *retrograde inversion*, which is based on a transposed version of the inversion but in reverse order.

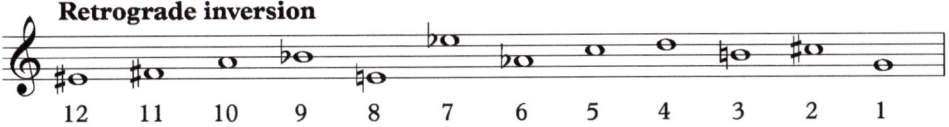

This is also divided into four short phrases, each starting with a rest.

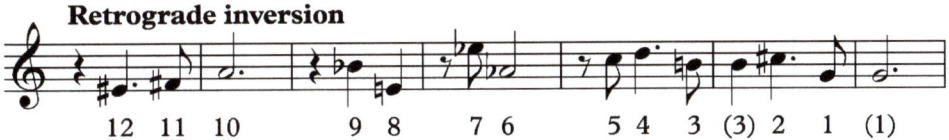

And, just as different permutations of the note row can be transposed or moved into different octaves for melodic interest, the same can be done when creating chords. Looking at the opening of Schönberg's theme, you will notice that while the cellos are playing a melody based on the original twelve-note row, the woodwind and harp are providing an accompaniment based on chords created from a transposition of the note row.

ACTIVITY:

Listen to the complete theme from Schönberg's *Variations for Orchestra*, noticing that the four permutations of the twelve-note row: Original – Retrograde Inversion – Retrograde – Inversion.

THINGS TO DO AND THINK ABOUT

Composing a serial melody

Create a tone row / note row, using each of the twelve notes of the chromatic scale, remembering to use each note once only.

Create a serial melody using the different permutations of your note row. Try to vary the rhythm to make your melody more interesting.

 **DON'T FORGET**

Inversion is when a melodic phrase is turned upside down, creating a mirror immage of the original phrase.

 ONLINE

Listen to the theme from *Variations for Orchestra* by clicking the link on the Digital Zone at www.brightredbooks.net/subjects.

 ONLINE TEST

To take an online test on this topic, go to the Digital Zone at www.brightredbooks.net/subjects.

43

MUSIC STYLES

SERIAL MUSIC 2

You will now explore the work of two composers who were pupils of Schönberg. Berg and Webern both adopted Schönberg's ideas about serial music, although they approached it in very different ways with completely different results. Berg's music is expansive and lyrical, using serial techniques in a way that still sometimes sounds tonal, whereas Webern's music is more dissonant and atonal.

Berg's *Violin Concerto* demonstrates his freer approach to serial music, which was not quite as strict as Schönberg. Berg created a note row but decided to arrange the twelve notes of the chromatic scale in a particular order. Notice that the first nine notes rise by the interval of a 3rd. However, unlike Schönberg's atonal note row, Berg arranges most of the notes in groups that outline major or minor chords.

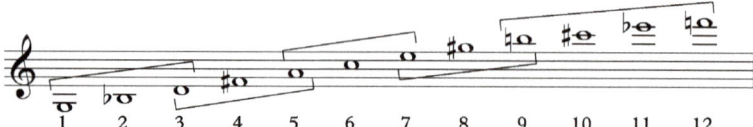

- Notes 1, 2 and 3 outline the chord of G minor.
- Notes 3, 4 and 5 outline the chord of D major.
- Notes 5, 6 and 7 outline the chord of A minor.
- Notes 7, 8 and 9 outline the chord of E major.
- Notes 9, 10, 11 and 12 form part of the whole-tone scale.
  This four-note motif matches the opening of a chorale melody by Bach, from his *Cantata No. 60 Es ist genug* (*It is enough*). It becomes significant towards the end of the final movement as Berg quotes the chorale melody.

ACTIVITY:

The following analysis looks at sections of two different movements from Berg's *Violin Concerto*. The first movement opens with the clarinet and harp playing arpeggio patterns, alternating with the solo violin. The arpeggios draw on Berg's original note row but using alternating notes, and making prominent use of the interval of the 5th.

This is followed by a short chordal section featuring violas and bassoons playing a syncopated rhythm, over longer notes played by the double bass. These chords are also based on the notes of the twelve-note row but arranged vertically to create the harmony. The double bass part is notated here with the abbreviation *8vb*.

The violin then plays an expressive ascending phrase based on the entire twelve-note row. It ends with a huge leap down to E natural and then a fall of a semitone down to E flat, suggesting a musical 'sigh'.

contd

44

Music styles: Serial music 2

In the final movement, Berg creates a solemn mood by incorporating the chorale melody from Bach's *Cantata No. 60*. You can see the original German words under the notes, with an English translation in brackets. The words suggest resignation and acceptance of death. Notice that the first four notes of the melody move by whole tones, corresponding to notes 9, 10, 11 and 12 of Berg's twelve-note row. The solo violin plays the melody, accompanied by gentle chords on the violins and violas, along with a countermelody on the bassoon.

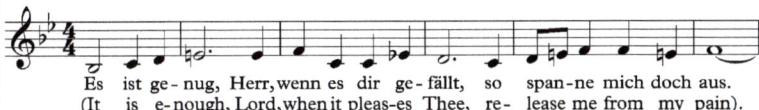

This is followed by some gentle interplay between the solo violin and clarinets, with the clarinets playing the chorale melody using Bach's original harmonies with a homophonic texture.

The texture then becomes more antiphonal as the melody is shared between the solo violin and clarinets.

Towards the end of the music a rich harmonisation of the chorale is played by the woodwind, and later joined by the strings. The solo violin soars high above the rest of the orchestra, as if entering heaven. The music finishes pianissimo.

Webern's approach to serial music was quite different. Rather than featuring expansive or expressive melodies, Webern's music is often fragmented, generally making use of short motifs with little or no repetition. The *Variations for Piano* demonstrates Webern's individual approach to serial music. The third movement is based on a twelve-note row, not unlike the kind of atonal note row that Schönberg might have used.

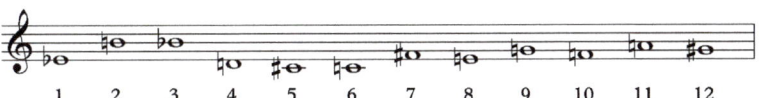

The opening bars of the music show all twelve notes of the note row being used in order. Rather than creating a specific melody, however, Webern avoids any sense of melodic shape by distributing the notes of his note row across different octaves. A prominent feature of the music, therefore, is the use of wide leaps and disjointed rhythms.

As the music progresses there are many discords using large intervals such as 7ths and 9ths. There are also some sudden changes in the level of the dynamics.

THINGS TO DO AND THINK ABOUT

Developing your serial composition

You might consider developing a serial composition by experimenting with different melodic intervals, exploring different rhythm.

DON'T FORGET

8vb is an abbreviation for the Italian term 'ottava bassa', indicating that the notes should be played an octave lower than written on the stave.

ONLINE

Listen to the opening of Berg's *Violin Concerto* by clicking the link on the Digital Zone at www.brightredbooks.net/subjects.

DON'T FORGET

An antiphonal texture is when two or more groups of instruments or voices alternate to create a question-and-answer effect.

ONLINE

Listen to the ending of Berg's *Violin Concerto* by clicking the link on the Digital Zone at www.brightredbooks.net/subjects.

ONLINE

Listen to the third movement from Webern's *Variations for Piano* by clicking the link on the Digital Zone at www.brightredbooks.net/subjects.

ONLINE TEST

To take an online test on this topic, go to the Digital Zone at www.brightredbooks.net/subjects.

MUSIC STYLES
NEOCLASSICAL MUSIC

Neoclassical (or *new classical*) is a style of music that emerged in the early part of the twentieth century, mainly as a reaction against the lush and chromatic style of nineteenth-century Romantic music. Large orchestral forces and complex textures were replaced by smaller ensembles and simpler textures. Some composers based their music on forms and structures from earlier styles such as Renaissance, Baroque or Classical music. Neoclassical music still has a distinct twentieth-century sound, however, often featuring abrupt modulations, unexpected melodic twists and unusual harmonies.

THE MAIN CHARACTERISTICS OF NEOCLASSICAL MUSIC

The table below outlines the main characteristics of Neoclassical music.

Style/form	Based on Renaissance dances, Baroque contrapuntal textures, or Classical styles such as symphony or concerto
Melodic	Clear-cut melodic phrases, but with unusual or unexpected twists Use of repetition and sequence
Harmonic	Tonal harmony, but with some discords or sudden key changes
Rhythmic	Generally straightforward rhythms Some use of syncopation or time changes
Structural	Use of Baroque and Classical forms such as binary, ternary, concerto grosso, ground bass and passacaglia
Timbre	Small orchestras and instrumental ensembles Some unusual combination of instruments or varied playing techniques

Warlock's *Capriol Suite*

Warlock's *Capriol Suite* is a collection of six short movements inspired by Renaissance dances. The second movement, *Pavane*, is based on a Renaissance pavan.

The music is played by a string orchestra, has two beats in the bar, a homophonic texture, and is in binary form. It starts with the violas providing a rhythmic ostinato accompaniment – the kind of rhythm featured in Renaissance dances, usually played on a percussion instrument such as a tambourine, tabor or tambour.

The violins then play the melody of section A, starting in a minor key and modulating to the relative major. Section B starts in the relative major key but returns to the minor key, ending with a tierce di Picardie.

This is all repeated, but with the cellos playing the melody while the violins and violas play a descant, and the double basses play the ostinato accompaniment. The fuller harmonies here are more characteristic of Neoclassical music than Renaissance music.

Finally, the ostinato rhythm is taken over by the violas and cellos for a short coda with a rallentando. The music ends pianissimo.

DON'T FORGET

A pavan is a Renaissance dance, with a feeling of two or four beats in a bar.

DON'T FORGET

A tierce de Picardie is when a major chord is heard at the end of a section of music in a minor key.

ONLINE

Listen to *Pavane* by clicking the link on the Digital Zone at www.brightredbooks.net/subjects.

contd

Music styles: Neoclassical music

Stravinsky's *Pulcinella*

Stravinsky's music for the ballet *Pulcinella* draws on forms and textures associated with Baroque music. Stravinsky also uses melodies that were originally thought to have been written by the Baroque composer Pergolesi, although it is now thought that some of the melodies may have been written by different composers. Nevertheless, Stravinsky adapted these Baroque themes into his own Neoclassical style. He uses Baroque forms and structures, but combines them with twentieth-century harmonies and rhythms.

ACTIVITY:

The opening movement, *Sinfonia (Overture)*, is in a Baroque concerto grosso style, setting a group of solo string instruments against the full string orchestra. Individual wind instruments are also featured.

The opening rhythmical theme, played by the full orchestra, starts with an anacrusis. It features dotted rhythms, syncopation and trills. There are also solo passages for the oboe and bassoon, featuring imitation and sequences. This is followed by a passage for the solo string group, featuring offbeat rhythms and time changes, and then a short passage for bassoons and oboes. After the main theme is played by the full orchestra again, solo passages are heard on the cello, violin, French horns and bassoons.

Prokofiev's *Classical Symphony*

Prokofiev's *Classical Symphony* is a deliberate attempt to imitate the graceful, elegant character of eighteenth-century Classical music. The symphony is in four movements and uses a small orchestra, in keeping with the Classical style. However, there are several sudden changes of key and unexpected melodic twists, placing the music firmly in the twentieth-century Neoclassical style.

ACTIVITY:

The third movement, *Gavotta*, is based on a gavotte – a dance dating back to the Baroque style. The music is in the key of D major, has four beats in a bar, and starts with an anacrusis. The overall form of the movement is ternary (ABA). Prominent features of the first section include octave leaps in the melody played by the upper strings, use of sequences, and some unexpected melodic and harmonic twists. These include an interrupted cadence at the end of the first four bars, and a sudden shift of key leading to a perfect cadence at the end of the section.

The middle section features a melody played by the woodwind, while the strings and timpani provide a drone and ostinato as an accompaniment. The section continues with a more elaborate melody on the oboe. The opening section returns but is now slower and quieter. The melody is now played by the flute accompanied by pizzicato strings. The last phrase is played by arco strings, ending with a perfect cadence played by pizzicato strings.

THINGS TO DO AND THINK ABOUT

Listen to other examples of Neoclassical music, and consider the following questions.

- Which style is the music based on?
- What instruments, and playing techniques, are used in the music?
- Which melodic, rhythmic or harmonic features suggest the music is Neoclassical?
- Are there any other important features or prominent concepts in the music?

DON'T FORGET

A concerto grosso is a piece of music for a group of solo instruments (concertino) with a string orchestra (ripieno).

ONLINE

Listen to *Sinfonia (Overture)* by clicking the link on the Digital Zone at www.brightredbooks.net/subjects.

DON'T FORGET

An interrupted cadence is formed by chords V–VI, and a perfect cadence is formed by chords V–I.

DON'T FORGET

A drone is a note held on, or repeated, in the bass. An ostinato is a short musical phrase or pattern repeated many times.

ONLINE

Listen to *Gavotta* by clicking the link on the Digital Zone at www.brightredbooks.net/subjects.

ONLINE

Listen to examples of Neoclassical music by clicking the links on the Digital Zone at www.brightredbooks.net/subjects.

MUSIC STYLES
BITONALITY AND POLYTONALITY

Tonality usually refers to music being in a particular key in which a tonic note (or keynote) is regarded as the most important note and the tonic chord is regarded as the most important chord. A piece of music might, for example, be in the key of G major (with the note G being the tonic note and the chord of G major being the tonic chord) or in the key of D minor (with the note D being the tonic note and the chord of D minor being the tonic chord). The term 'tonality' can also be used more generally. For example, a piece of music might be said to have either a major or minor tonality, meaning that it sounds either major or minor overall.

Some composers, particularly in the twentieth century, have used different types of scales such as modes or whole-tone scales, making tonality vague and more difficult to identify. Other composers have deliberately avoided tonality altogether by composing atonal music. In the early twentieth century composers also experimented with different types of tonality, such as **bitonality** and **polytonality**, in which different keys are used at the same time.

DON'T FORGET

Atonal music is music that has no sense of being in a major or minor key.

Béla Bartók (1881–1945)

BITONALITY

Bitonality is the term used to describe the use of two keys simultaneously. This might involve two instruments playing in different keys, or the right- and left-hand parts of the piano playing in different keys.

Boating is a piano piece by Bartók which begins with the left hand playing an ostinato pattern using only the white notes. The right hand then joins in playing a melody based on a pentatonic scale, using only the five black notes. While these two ideas are both quite simple, the overall effect sounds dissonant at times. As the music continues, try to listen out for what is being played by each hand separately.

ONLINE

Listen to *Boating* by clicking the link on the Digital Zone at www.brightredbooks.net/subjects.

DON'T FORGET

Bitonality is the use of two keys simultaneously.

DON'T FORGET

A tritone is an interval of three whole tones, making the interval of an augmented 4th.

Stravinsky uses bitonality for dramatic effect in his ballets *Petrushka* and *The Rite of Spring*. *Petrushka* tells the story of the loves and jealousies of three puppet figures from Russian folklore. The character Petrushka, often depicted as a jester or a clown, is in love with a ballerina. His love is not returned, however, and he feels the pain of rejection.

In the second scene of the ballet, Petrushka is thrown into the corner of a room. The music starts with a drum roll followed by dramatic bursts from the orchestra. Petrushka picks himself up and begins to dance. His conflicting feelings of love and rejection are depicted by two clarinets playing in different keys, which are a tritone apart. Clarinet 1 plays a phrase based on the notes of the C major chord, while clarinet 2 plays a similar phrase using the notes of the F sharp major chord. As the music continues, the use of instruments is vivid, with complex rhythms and harmonies, and several changes in tempo and time signature.

ONLINE

Listen to *Petrushka, Scene II* by clicking the link on the Digital Zone at www.brightredbooks.net/subjects.

Music styles: Bitonality and polytonality

POLYTONALITY

Polytonality is the term used to describe two or more keys used simultaneously. It is used to create an interesting effect in Ravel's *Boléro*. The entire piece is based on a repeating melody over an ostinato rhythm. To add interest, the melody is repeated by solo instruments and various combinations of instruments using different playing techniques. The music starts with an ostinato rhythm played on the snare drum, accompanied by gentle pizzicato notes on the violas and cellos.

The first part of the melody is played by a flute and repeated by a clarinet.

This is followed by the second part of the melody played by a bassoon and repeated at a high pitch by another clarinet. The first part of the melody is then played by an oboe and repeated by the unusual combination of flute and muted trumpet. The second part of the melody is played by a tenor saxophone and repeated by the high-pitched sopranino saxophone. The first part of the melody is then heard again, this time played by a combination of two piccolos, French horn and celesta, all playing in different keys. Piccolo 1 is in the key of E major, piccolo 2 is in G major, and both the French horn and the celeste are in C major. As all the instruments are playing the same melody, this use of polytonality creates a dissonant effect, with the melody sounding slightly out of tune.

In *Three Pieces for String Quartet, No. 1*, Stravinsky uses contrasting textures to emphasise the use of polytonality. Sometimes a tonic is suggested by using part of a scale, or by either a sustained or a repeated note. Following an introductory chord, featuring a harmonic effect on the viola, the first violin plays a rhythmical dance-like melody. Although there is no key signature, the four-note melody is centred on G and suggests the key of G major. Prominent rhythmic features of this melody are syncopation and changing time signatures. The viola sustains the note D throughout, and plays a repeated pizzicato D, which also suggests that D is a tonic note. The cello plays an ostinato figure prominently featuring the note D flat, suggesting D flat as another tonic. The second violin repeatedly enters with a short descending phrase in the key of C sharp minor. As C sharp is the enharmonic equivalent of D flat, both the second violin and cello could be regarded as sounding in the same key.

 **DON'T FORGET**

Polytonality is the simultaneous use of two or more keys.

 ONLINE

Listen to *Boléro* by clicking the link on the Digital Zone at www.brightredbooks.net/subjects.

 **DON'T FORGET**

An enharmonic equivalent is when a note is called a different name but sounds the same. For example, D♭ (D flat) sounds the same as C# (C sharp).

 ONLINE

Listen to *Three Pieces for String Quartet, No. 1* by clicking the link on the Digital Zone at www.brightredbooks.net/subjects.

THINGS TO DO AND THINK ABOUT

Explore bitonality or polytonality by playing the same melody in two different keys at the same time, or by creating an accompaniment in a different key from the melody.

MUSIC LITERACY

CONCEPTS

Music literacy is about understanding music notation. You will have opportunities to explore many of the music literacy concepts through performing, listening and creating your own music. The music literacy concepts for Advanced Higher Music build on previous knowledge and understanding of concepts at lower levels. You Can find a table with all the music literacy concepts that are introduced at Advanced Higher on page 5 of this study guide.

DON'T FORGET

You can revise concepts from previous levels by referring to the Bright Red N5 and Higher music study guides.

Treble clef and bass clef

In standard music notation, notes are written on five lines and four spaces called a stave or a staff, with a clef at the beginning. You will already be familiar with the notes on both the treble clef and bass clef staves, including the use of ledger lines. For Advanced Higher, you may be asked to identify or write notes up to two ledger lines above or below each stave.

For the treble clef, this would include A and B below middle C (using up to two ledger lines below the stave) and high B and C (using up to two ledger lines above the stave).

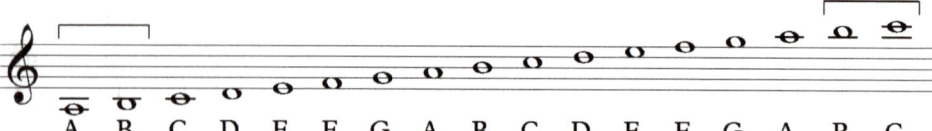

The additional bass clef notes you will need to know are low C and D (up to two ledger lines below the stave) and high D and E (up to two ledger lines above the stave).

Working between the treble clef and bass clef

For Higher Music you were required transpose notes down one octave from the treble clef into the bass clef. In the Advanced Higher Music question paper, you may be required you do either of the following.

- Transpose notes up one octave from the bass clef to the treble clef.
- Rewrite (in either treble or bass clef) a note at the same pitch using up to two ledger lines below or above the stave.

The following examples show groups of notes using up to two ledger lines below or above the stave, transposed up or down an octave, and rewritten at the same pitch.

- Here are notes A, B, C, D and E as they would be written at the higher end of the bass clef, using two ledger lines above the stave. Notice that the third note is middle C, with A and B being below middle C, and D and E being above middle C.

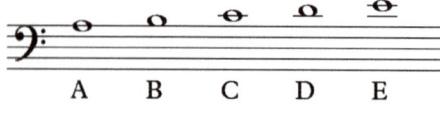

- Here are the same notes rewritten at the same pitch at the lower end of the treble clef, using two ledger lines below the stave. Notice that the third note is still middle C, with A and B being below middle C, and D and E being above middle C.

- Here is the original group of notes, now transposed up one octave from the bass clef to treble clef.

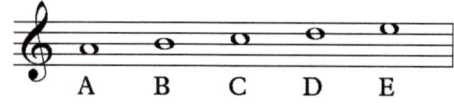

50

contd

Music Literacy: Concepts

In some cases, you will only be asked to rewrite or transpose one or two notes. However, there may be occasions when you are required to write a short phrase. The following examples of melodic phrases written in one clef, then rewritten at the same pitch in the other clef and transposed up one octave into the treble clef, illustrate some other points to be aware of.

- Here is a short phrase in the key of D major written in the bass clef.

- Here is the same phrase rewritten at the same pitch in the treble clef. Remember to take note of any ledger lines that might be required, and make sure the stems go in the correct direction.

- Here is the same phrase transposed up an octave into the treble clef. Again, make sure the stems go in the correct direction.

- Here is a short phrase in the key of Bb major written in the treble clef.

- Here is the same phrase rewritten at the same pitch in the bass clef. As well as taking note of any ledger lines that might be required and making sure the stems go in the correct direction, you should also take care to beam any quavers correctly.

- Here is the same phrase transposed up an octave into the treble clef. Again, remember to make sure the stems go in the correct direction, and that any quavers are beamed correctly.

- Here is a short phrase in the key of C major written in the bass clef.

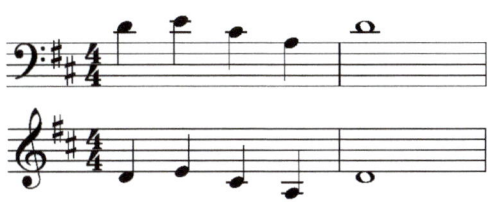

- Here is the same phrase rewritten at the same pitch in the treble clef. As this example is in compound time, remember to group and beam the quavers correctly. Also, if there are any dotted notes, remember to place the dot clearly after the note head.

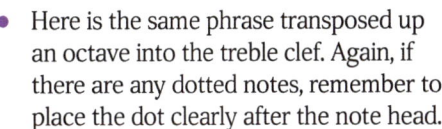

- Here is the same phrase transposed up an octave into the treble clef. Again, if there are any dotted notes, remember to place the dot clearly after the note head.

- Here is a short phrase in the key of D minor written in the bass clef.

- Here is the same phrase rewritten at the same pitch in the bass clef. As well as taking note of any ledger lines that are required and making sure the stems go in the correct direction, you should also check that any accidentals are written clearly before the appropriate note head.

- Here is the same phrase transposed up an octave into the treble clef. Again, take particular care to ensure that any accidentals are placed correctly before the appropriate note on the appropriate line or space.

🌧️ THINGS TO DO AND THINK ABOUT

Referring to a piece of music that you are playing or singing, look for a short phrase or even just a few notes that fall around middle C, maybe just going a note or two above or below middle C. Write out the same phrase, or group of notes, in both the treble clef and the bass clef, taking care to write them at the same pitch. Once you have done that, write the same phrase, or group of notes, an octave higher in the treble clef.

 DON'T FORGET

Pay particular attention to any ledger lines, and make sure the stems go in the correct direction.

 **ONLINE TEST**

To take an online test on this topic, go to the Digital Zone at www.brightredbooks.net/subjects.

DON'T FORGET

Group and beam any quavers correctly and make sure that the stems go in the correct direction. For any dotted notes, the dot should be written immediately after the appropriate note head. Any accidentals should be written immediately before the appropriate note head on the appropriate line or space.

51

MUSIC LITERACY
SCALES AND KEY SIGNATURES

You will already be aware of the scales and key signatures for the keys of C major, G major, F major and A minor. The new scales and key signatures introduced at Advanced Higher are **D major**, **B flat major**, **E minor** and **D minor**.

SCALES OF D MAJOR AND B FLAT MAJOR

The numbers of each note of the scale (known as the degrees of the scale) are shown below the notes. The notes that have sharps or flats are indicated by the square brackets above the stave. Accidentals are not required for any flats or sharps that appear in the key signature. They are shown here, in brackets, just as a reminder of which notes are affected by the key signature.

The key signature of D major has two sharps (F# and C#).

The scale of D major:

The scale of B flat major:

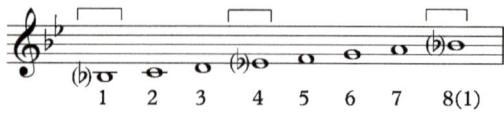

DON'T FORGET

The key signature of B flat major has two flats (B♭ and E♭).

SCALES OF E MINOR AND D MINOR

There are two different kinds of minor scale: the *harmonic* minor and the *melodic* minor. The harmonic minor scale, like the major scale, is the same both ascending and descending. The melodic minor scale, however, is not the same ascending and descending.

In the harmonic minor scale, the 7th note (or 7th degree of the scale) is raised by a semitone. This is the same whether the scale is ascending or descending.

In the melodic minor scale, both the 6th and 7th notes are raised by a semitone when the notes are ascending, but are restored to their original pitch when the notes are descending.

E minor

In the ascending form of the E harmonic minor scale, the 7th note (D) is raised to D sharp and requires a sharp sign (#) as an accidental. The 2nd note (F sharp) does not require an accidental, as F sharp appears in the key signature.

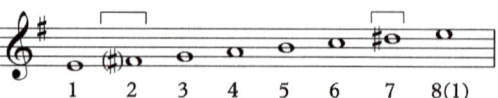

In the descending form of the E harmonic minor scale, the 7th degree of the scale (D) is still raised by a semitone to D sharp. The 2nd degree of the scale (F sharp) again does not require an accidental as F sharp appears in the key signature.

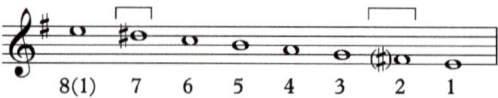

In the ascending form of the E melodic minor scale, the 6th note (C) is raised to C sharp and the 7th note (D) is raised to D sharp. The 2nd note (F sharp) does not require an accidental as F sharp appears in the key signature.

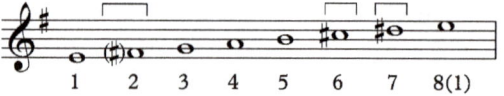

52

Music Literacy: Scales and key signatures

In the descending form of the E melodic minor scale, however, the 6th degree of the scale remains as C natural and the 7th degree remains as D natural. The 2nd note remains as F sharp as F sharp appears in the key signature.

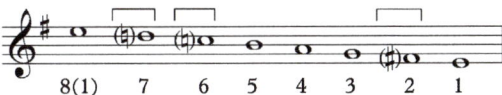

D minor

In the ascending form of the D harmonic minor scale, the 7th degree of the scale is raised by a semitone, therefore the note C is raised to C sharp. The 6th note (B flat) does not require a flat sign (♭) as an accidental, as B flat appears in the key signature. It is shown here in brackets just as a reminder.

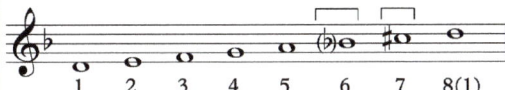

In the descending form of the D harmonic minor scale, the 7th degree of the scale is still raised by a semitone to C sharp, and the 6th degree is still B flat as B flat appears in the key signature.

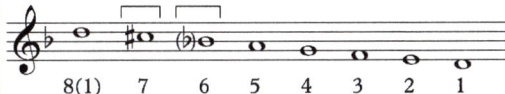

In the ascending form of the D melodic minor scale, the 6th note (B flat) is raised to B natural and the 7th note (C) is raised to C sharp.

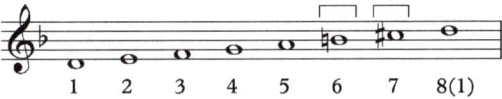

In the descending form of the D melodic minor, the 6th degree of the scale remains as B flat and the 7th degree remains as C natural. Generally, no accidentals would be required as B flat is already in the key signature and C natural is not affected by the key signature.

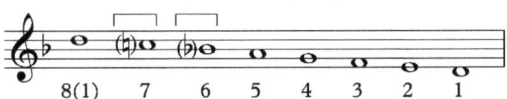

ENHARMONIC EQUIVALENT

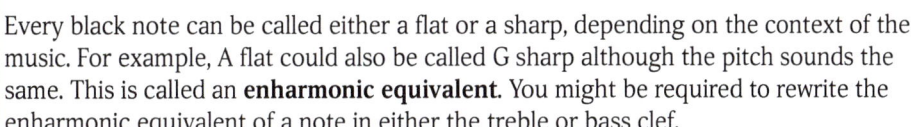

Notes in music can be known by more than one name. This can be seen most simply, and most obviously, by looking at the layout of the black notes on a piano keyboard.

Every black note can be called either a flat or a sharp, depending on the context of the music. For example, A flat could also be called G sharp although the pitch sounds the same. This is called an **enharmonic equivalent**. You might be required to rewrite the enharmonic equivalent of a note in either the treble or bass clef.

💭 THINGS TO DO AND THINK ABOUT

Look at the music notation for any pieces or songs that you are performing and try to answer the following questions.
- What key is the music in? Is it major or minor?
- If the music is in a minor key, which notes suggest this? Look out for the 6th and 7th degrees of the scale.
- If the music is in a minor key, can you identify any elements of either the harmonic or melodic minor scale?

Look at the music notation for some pieces or songs that you are not familiar with and try to answer the same questions.

DON'T FORGET

In the harmonic minor scale, the 7th note is raised by a semitone. This is the same for both the ascending and descending form of the scale.

DON'T FORGET

In the melodic minor scale, both the 6th and 7th notes are raised by a semitone when the notes are ascending and lowered by a semitone when the notes are descending.

DON'T FORGET

An enharmonic equivalent is when a note is written and called a different name but sounds the same. For example, E♭ (E flat) can also be written as D# (D sharp).

ONLINE TEST

To take an online test on this topic, go to the Digital Zone at www.brightredbooks.net/subjects.

53

MUSIC LITERACY
CHORDS AND INVERSIONS

TRIADS

You will already be familiar with chords I, IV, V and VI in the keys of C major, G major, F major and A minor. These three-note chords are called **triads** and are made up of the 1st, 3rd and 5th notes of a scale. For example, in the scale of C major, the 1st note is C, the 3rd note is E and the 5th note is G.

The 1st, 3rd and 5th notes make up the triad of C major. The root note here is C and when the root note is the lowest note of the chord it is said to be in *root position*.

If the 3rd is the lowest note the chord is said to be in 1st inversion, and if the 5th is the lowest note the chord is said to be in 2nd inversion. Lower case letters 'a', 'b' and 'c' are commonly used to identify chords in root position, 1st inversion and 2nd inversion. The letter 'a' indicates root position, 'b' indicates 1st inversion and 'c' indicates 2nd inversion. The letter 'a' is often omitted, however, as it is commonly accepted that a chord with no letter is in root position.

> **DON'T FORGET**
> Make sure that you can tell the difference between the root position, 1st inversion and 2nd inversion of a chord.

In the key of C major the chord of C major is chord I. In root position the note C would be in the bass and there is no need to use the letter 'a'. In 1st inversion the 3rd (E) would be in the bass. This could be identified either by the chord symbol C/E (indicating the chord of C major with the note E in the bass), or the Roman numeral and letter 'Ib' (indicating chord I in 1st inversion). In 2nd inversion the 5th (G) would be in the bass. This could be identified either by the chord symbol C/G (indicating the chord of C major with the note G in the bass), or the Roman numeral and letter 'Ic' (indicating chord I in 2nd inversion).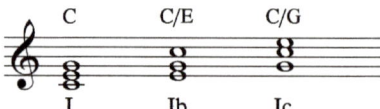

Very often the notes of chords are split between the treble and bass clef with the chords containing four notes, meaning that one or more notes of the triad would be doubled. This makes no difference to the inversion, however, as the inversion is defined by the lowest note of the chord.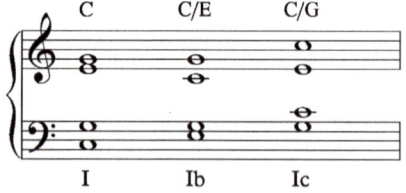

> **DON'T FORGET**
> The lowest note of a chord will often be notated in the bass clef.

CHORD PROGRESSIONS AND CADENCES

Inversions of chords can be used to create more movement in the bass, or to make a chord progression sound more interesting without changing the harmonies frequently. This example is in the key of G major. The chord names are shown above the melody, while the Roman numerals and position of the chords are indicated below the moving bass line. The last three chords (Ic–V–I) form a common progression for a perfect cadence.

As well as chords I, IV, V and VI, you will also need to be able to recognise chord II and chord V7 (dominant 7th).

Chord II is built on the second note of the scale. In a major key, chord II is a minor chord; in a minor key, chord II is a diminished chord. For example, chord II in the key of C major would be built on the 2nd note of the scale (D) and would be the chord of D minor.

contd

54

Music Literacy: Chords and inversions

In the key of A minor, chord II would be built on the 2nd note of the scale (B) and would be the chord of B diminished.

Chord V7, like chord V, is built on the 5th note of the scale. However, as well as containing the root, 3rd and 5th notes of the scale, chord V7 also contains the 7th note of the scale to make it the dominant 7th. For example, in the key of C major, chord V would be built on the 5th (dominant) note of the C major scale. Starting from the dominant note (G), chord V would contain the notes G, B and D. However, chord V7 would also contain the 7th note (F) from the root, making it the dominant 7th (G7).

Chord IIb (the 2nd inversion of chord II) followed by chord V7 (the dominant 7th) is also a common combination of chords at a cadence point. This example is in the key of F major. The chord names are shown above the melody and the Roman numerals and position of the chords are indicated below the mainly descending bass line. The last three chords (IIb–V7–I) form another common progression for a perfect cadence.

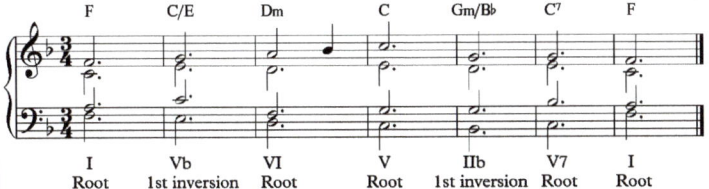

DON'T FORGET
Chord V7 is also known as the dominant 7th.

DON'T FORGET
Always establish what key the music is in before you start to identify the chords.

OTHER CADENCES

An imperfect cadence always ends with chord V. This example is in the key of A minor and consists of chord VI followed by chord V, both in root position.

A plagal cadence is always formed by chord IV followed by chord I. It is sometimes referred to as an 'Amen' cadence as many hymn-tunes end with a plagal cadence. This example is in the key of F major and ends with chord IV followed by chord I, both in root position.

An interrupted cadence is formed by chord V followed by chord VI. It is sometime referred to as a 'surprise' cadence because the listener often expects to hear chord I at the end, therefore chord VI is unexpected. In a major key, chord VI is a minor chord; in a minor key, chord VI is a major chord.

This example of an interrupted cadence is in the key of G major and consists of chords IIb, V7 (the dominant 7th) and VI.

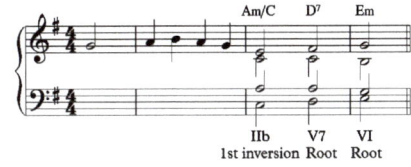

This example of an interrupted cadence is in the key of D minor and consists of chords Ic, V7 (the dominant 7th) and VI.

ONLINE TEST
To take an online test on this topic, go to the Digital Zone at www.brightredbooks.net/subjects.

DON'T FORGET
In a major key, chord VI is a minor chord and, in a minor key, chord VI is a major chord.

ONLINE
Go online to the Digital Zone and click the link to listen to *Wohin?* At www.brightredbooks.net/subjects.

THINGS TO DO AND THINK ABOUT

Analyse a chord progression in a piece of music or a song that you are performing. If you play a melody instrument, or sing, there will usually be a piano accompaniment part containing chords.

55

MUSIC LITERACY

MORE CHORDS AND INTERVALS

For Higher Music you were required to identify dominant 7th, diminished triad, diminished 7th and added 6th chords by their sound. For Advanced Higher you will also be required to recognise and write these chords in music notation. In addition, you will be required to recognise the augmented triad, as well as intervals of the augmented 4th and diminished 5th.

DON'T FORGET

The dominant 7th chord (V7) is often followed by the tonic chord (I) to form a perfect cadence.

ONLINE

Click the link on the Digital Zone to listen to examples of songs that use dominant 7th chords at www.brightredbooks.net/subjects.

DOMINANT 7TH

The **dominant 7th** chord is built on the dominant note of a scale with the 7th note added above its root. For example, in the key of C major, G is the dominant (5th) note of the scale. This means the dominant 7th chord (G7) would contain the notes G, B, D and F. Here are examples of dominant 7th chords based on C, F and G.

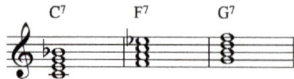

DIMINISHED TRIAD AND DIMINISHED 7TH

A **diminished triad** is a minor triad with the 5th lowered by a semitone. This means that the interval between the lowest and highest notes of the triad is a **diminished 5th**.

For example, the C minor triad contains the root (C), the minor 3rd (E flat) and the perfect 5th (G), while the C diminished triad contains the root (C), the minor 3rd (E flat), and the diminished 5th (G flat).

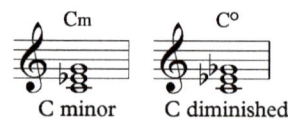

Here are the triads of E diminished, B diminished and G sharp diminished, using common symbols.

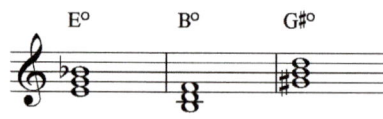

A **diminished 7th** chord is a diminished triad with the interval of the diminished 7th added, the interval between the lowest and highest notes being a diminished 7th. For example, a diminished triad based on B would contain the root (B), the minor 3rd (D) and the diminished 5th (F), while the diminished 7th chord would contain the root (B), the minor 3rd (D), the diminished 5th (F) and the diminished 7th (A flat).

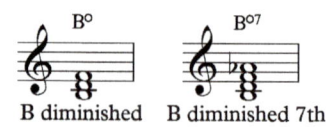

DON'T FORGET

An enharmonic equivalent is when a note is written and called a different name but sounds the same. For example, D♭ (D flat) could also be written as C# (C sharp) as it sounds the same.

However, in music notation the diminished 7th note is sometimes written as an enharmonic equivalent. This means that, in the case of B diminished 7th, the A flat might be written as a G sharp. While this is not technically a diminished 7th interval, it sounds the same because G sharp is the enharmonic equivalent of A flat. Therefore, the same chord could be notated with the notes B, D, F and G sharp.

Here are the chords E diminished 7th, B diminished 7th and G sharp diminished 7th, using common symbols.

DON'T FORGET

Sforzando (*sfz*) is an Italian term that literally means 'forcing' and describes a note or chord being played with a sudden accent or emphasis.

The diminished triad and diminished 7th chord can be harmonically ambiguous, so they are often used either to create tension or to modulate to an unrelated key. Examples of diminished triads and a diminished 7th chord can be found in the song *The Stormy Morning* by Schubert. The piano introduction, in the key of D minor, features a diminished 7th chord played sforzando (*sfz*) in the second bar (a), creating a slightly unsettled effect. However, the third bar ends with a perfect cadence in the key of D minor (b), providing a sense of 'returning home'.

contd

Music Literacy: More chords and intervals

This next phrase, which comes after the second verse and at the end of the song, features a descending triplet figure based on diminished triads (a). The left hand also outlines a rising diminished 7th chord, with the G sharp being the enharmonic equivalent of A flat (b). The phrase ends with a perfect cadence in the key of D minor (c).

ADDED 6TH

An **added 6th** chord is a triad with the 6th note added above the root. For example, the three major triads of C, F and G each contain three notes – the root, 3rd and 5th.

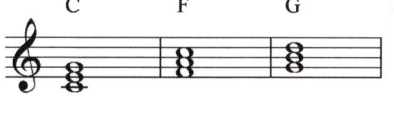

If the 6th note from the root is added above each triad this would create an added 6th chord.

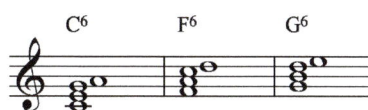

The added 6th chord is slightly richer and sweeter sounding and is often used in jazz and other styles of popular music.

AUGMENTED TRIAD

An **augmented triad** is a major triad with the 5th raised by a semitone. This means that the interval between the lowest and highest notes of the triad is an augmented 5th.

For example, the C major triad contains the root (C), the major 3rd (E) and the perfect 5th (G), while the C augmented triad contains the root (C), the major 3rd (E) and the augmented 5th (G sharp).

TRITONE AND AUGMENTED 4TH

A **tritone** is an interval of three whole tones, making the interval of an **augmented 4th**. For example, starting on C and moving up in steps of whole tones, the fourth note (F sharp) would be the tritone (i.e. three tones above C).

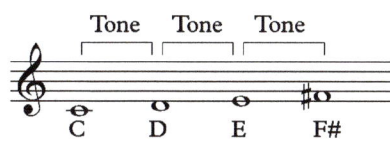

The tritone (augmented 4th) can be used as either a melodic or a harmonic interval.

The interval of the diminished 5th is the enharmonic equivalent of the augmented 4th. Although written differently, they sound the same.

:cloud: THINGS TO DO AND THINK ABOUT

Experiment with playing different chords, such as the added 6th, dominant 7th, diminished triad, diminished 7th and the augmented triad, trying to get to know how they sound. Consider how you might incorporate any of them into your own composition.

 DON'T FORGET

A triplet is a group of three notes played in the time of two.

 ONLINE

Listen to Schubert's *The Stormy Morning* by clicking the link on the Digital Zone at www.brightredbooks.net/subjects.

 ONLINE

Listen to examples of songs that use diminished 7th chords at www.brightredbooks.net/subjects.

 DON'T FORGET

The four strings of a ukulele are tuned to the notes of an added 6th chord (C, E, G and A).

 ONLINE

Listen to examples of songs that use added 6th chords at www.brightredbooks.net/subjects.

 ONLINE

Listen to examples of songs that use augmented chords at www.brightredbooks.net/subjects.

 DON'T FORGET

A tritone is the interval of the augmented 4th, which is made up of three whole tones.

 ONLINE TEST

To take an online test on this topic, go to the Digital Zone at www.brightredbooks.net/subjects.

57

MUSIC LITERACY

RHYTHM

You will already be familiar with many rhythm concepts from N5 and Higher, some of which can be recognised from listening to music and others that can be identified in music notation. The additional rhythm concepts that you need to be aware of in music notation for Advanced Higher are ties, syncopated rhythms, 5/4 time, and time changes.

DON'T FORGET

You will still need to know the rhythm/tempo concepts from N5 and Higher.

ONLINE

Listen to *When the Saints Go Marching In* by clicking the link on the Digital Zone at www.brightredbooks.net/subjects.

DON'T FORGET

A tie must link notes of the same pitch and should not be confused with a slur, which indicates that notes of different pitches should be played legato.

TIES

A **tie** is a curved line which links two notes of the same pitch. It means that when the first note is sounded, it is held on for the combined value of both notes. For example, two minims linked together by a tie would be equal in length to one semibreve.

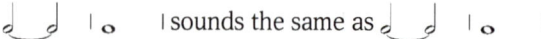 sounds the same as

Ties can be written either above or below the noteheads, depending on the position of the notes and stems on the stave. As a rule, notes below the middle line with the stems going up would have the tie below the noteheads.

Notes above the middle line with the stems going down would have the tie above the noteheads.

Ties are often used to join notes across bar lines, as in this example from *When the Saints Go Marching In*.

It is possible for a tie to join more than two notes. In this example, four notes are tied, lasting for a total of eleven beats.

SYNCOPATED RHYTHMS

Syncopation is a rhythmic feature where stronger accented notes are played on the weaker beats in a bar, or even between beats. For example, in 4/4 time the second beat might have the extra emphasis. This sometimes makes the music sound off the beat. **Syncopated rhythms** often feature a short note followed by a longer note, and then a short note again.

Syncopated rhythms can be found in different styles of music, but are a common feature of popular music styles including ragtime, jazz and swing. The ragtime music of Scott Joplin is known for its prominent use of syncopated rhythms.

The introduction to *The Cascades* begins with a syncopated rhythm based on a quaver–crotchet–quaver grouping.

ONLINE

Listen to Scott Joplin's *The Cascades* and *The Entertainer* by clicking the links on the Digital Zone at www.brightredbooks.net/subjects.

The melody of *The Entertainer* features a syncopated rhythm based on a semiquaver–quaver–semiquaver grouping, as well as tied notes.

Music Literacy: Rhythm

TIME SIGNATURE OF 5/4

5/4 is an example of an irregular time signature that does not fit into the pattern of either simple or compound time. Rather than having two, three or four beats in every bar, 5/4 time has five crotchet beats in each bar. It is sometimes helpful to subdivide the five beats into groups of two or three. This means the five beats could be counted as either 1–2–3–1–2 or 1–2–1–2–3. Although not a common time signature, examples of 5/4 time can be found in different styles of music.

The second movement of Tchaikovsky's Symphony No. 6, which is a Romantic orchestral work, is in 5/4 time. The opening theme, played by the cellos and then repeated by the woodwind, also features triplets. The phrasing in the music suggests a rhythmic feeling of 1–2–1–2–3, 1–2–1–2–3.

Take Five, performed the Dave Brubeck Quartet, is a jazz-style piece in 5/4 time, with a rhythmic feeling of 1–2–3–1–2, 1–2–3–1–2. The melody, with swung quavers, is played by the saxophone, accompanied by the piano, double bass and drum kit. The music also features improvisation.

In *Mars, the Bringer of War* from *The Planets* by Holst, the timpani, harp and strings play an ostinato rhythm in 5/4 time. The beginning of each bar also features triplets.

What makes Holst's music sound even more dramatic is that the string players use a technique called *col legno*, meaning that they strike the strings with the wood of the bow rather than drawing the hair of the bow across the strings.

TIME CHANGES

While many pieces of music have the same time signature throughout, it is possible for the time signature to change during the music. This is called a **time change**.

Composers sometimes use time changes to add rhythmic interest to their music.

The *Fantasia on a Theme of Thomas Tallis* by Vaughan Williams and the song *America* from the musical *West Side Story* both feature time changes. You will find examples of these in the Antiphonal Texture section of this guide.

The *Intermezzo Interrotto* from *Concerto for Orchestra* by Bartók consists of two themes, both of which feature several time changes and irregular time signatures. The music opens with the strings playing in unison/octaves followed by the first theme played by the oboe, then repeated by the rest of the woodwind.

The second theme is played by the violas, accompanied by the harp, and repeated by the violins.

THINGS TO DO AND THINK ABOUT

Experiment with using rhythmic features such as ties, syncopated rhythms, 5/4 time and time changes in your own composition.

DON'T FORGET

An ostinato is short melodic or rhythmic pattern that is repeated many times.

ONLINE

Listen to examples of music in 5/4 time by clicking the links on the Digital Zone at www.brightredbooks.net/subjects.

DON'T FORGET

Irregular time signatures often have five or seven beats in the bar.

ONLINE

Listen to *Intermezzo Interrotto* by clicking the link on the Digital Zone at www.brightredbooks.net/subjects.

ONLINE TEST

To take an online test on this topic, go to the Digital Zone at www.brightredbooks.net/subjects.

MUSIC LITERACY

SIGNS, SYMBOLS AND ABBREVIATIONS

When interpreting a composer's intentions from printed music, it is important not only to play or sing the correct notes with the correct rhythms but also to be aware of other signs, symbols and abbreviations that provide important information.

8VA AND 8VB

Performers are sometimes required to play notes that come above or below the stave. In music notation such notes are often written using ledger lines, although using several ledger lines can make the music difficult to read. To avoid this, notes can be written within the lines and spaces of the stave, but with an instruction to play them either an octave higher or an octave lower. Such instructions are shown in the music by the following abbreviations for Italian terms:

- *8va* (*ottava alta*), indicating the notes should be played an octave higher
- *8vb* (*ottava bassa*), indicating the notes should be played an octave lower.

The specific notes to be transposed are usually indicated by a dotted line.

Notes to be played an octave higher have the abbreviation *8va* along with a dotted line above the stave.

Notes to be played an octave lower have the abbreviation *8vb* along with a dotted line below the stave.

Sometimes the term 'loco' is used to cancel out a previous *8va* or *8vb* instruction, indicating that the music should now be played at the written pitch.

DON'T FORGET

8va indicates that notes should be played an octave higher than written.

DON'T FORGET

8vb indicates that notes should be played an octave lower than written.

DAL SEGNO (D.S.)

Start repeat: 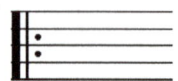   End repeat:

If a piece of music is to be repeated from the beginning, this might be indicated by the abbreviation D.C. (da capo). However, sometimes there is a requirement to repeat from a particular point in the music. In this case the Italian term **dal segno** (usually abbreviated to **D.S.**) is used to indicate the music should be repeated from a special sign.

The sign appears above the stave at the point where the music should be repeated from.

The abbreviation D.S. would usually appear at the end of the music, either above or below the stave, instructing the performer to go back to the sign.

DON'T FORGET

A repeat sign is a double bar line with two dots, indicating that a section of music should be played again.

FINE

The Italian term *Fine* simply means 'end' and is used to indicate where a piece of music or song finishes. It is common for the abbreviation D.S. to be combined with the term *Fine* to make the phrase **D.S. al Fine**. This instructs the performer to repeat from the sign and stop at the place marked *Fine*.

Fine appears at the end of the bar where the music should stop and is also indicated by a double bar line.

DON'T FORGET

Fine, meaning 'end', may appear anywhere in a piece of music. It can be written either above or below the stave.

60

Music Literacy: Signs, symbols and abbreviations

APPOGGIATURA

Sometimes referred to as a *leaning note*, an **appoggiatura** is an ornamental note that comes either a step above or a step below the main note and resolves onto the main note.

The opening notes of this example features an appoggiatura where the first note (G) does not belong to the chord of F major but resolves onto the second note (F), which does belong to the chord.

The *Adagietto* from Mahler's Symphony No. 5 features several appoggiaturas. At the start of the first full bar the first note (E) does not belong to the chord of F major but resolves onto the next note (F), which does belong to the chord. The start of the following bar also features an appoggiatura.

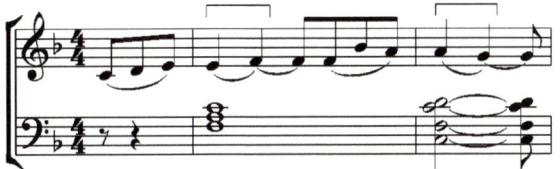

In some styles of music an appoggiatura might be notated as a small note, which takes half the value of the main note or two-thirds of the value if the main note is a dotted note.

For example, two crotchets could be notated as a small crotchet followed by a minim.

Played: Written:

 ONLINE

Listen to *Adagietto* by clicking the links on the Digital Zone at www.brightredbooks.net/subjects.

TURN

A **turn** is an ornament consisting of four notes which turn around a main note; starting with the note above, followed by the main note, then the note below, and returning to the main note. In music notation it is often indicted by a special symbol.

Played: Written:

A turn may also start after the main note, in which case the symbol is written after the main note.

Played: Written:

The rhythmic grouping of turns can vary, depending on the musical context and tempo, although the overall pattern remains the same. In the first movement of Beethoven's *Emperor* Piano Concerto, the first theme, makes prominent use of a turn featuring a triplet grouping.

 ONLINE TEST

To take an online test on this topic, go to the Digital Zone at www.brightredbooks.net/subjects.

DON'T FORGET

A turn is an ornament consisting of four notes - the note above the main note, the main note, the note below, and the main note again.

 ONLINE

Listen to Beethoven's *Emperor* Piano Concerto by clicking the link on the Digital Zone at www.brightredbooks.net/subjects.

 THINGS TO DO AND THINK ABOUT

Look at the music notation of pieces of music or songs you are performing and try to identify any signs, symbols or abbreviations, making sure you know what they mean.

61

COURSE ASSESSMENT

This section will provide you with more detailed information about the externally assessed components of the Advanced Higher Music exam, along with advice on how to prepare for each of them.

COURSE OVERVIEW

The Advanced Higher Music course consists of three mandatory components plus one optional component, all of which are externally assessed.

MANDATORY COMPONENTS

The three mandatory components are the Question Paper, the Assignment and Performance on one instrument or voice. For the optional component there is a choice between either Performance on a second instrument, or voice, or submitting a Portfolio of compositions and/or arrangements. A total of 120 marks are available, scaled to a mark out of 100.

The tables provide a summary of the three mandatory components and choice of optional components, showing how each one will be assessed, the total number of marks available for each component, and the scaled mark.

Mandatory components	How it will be assessed	Marks available	Scaled mark
Question paper	Written examination based on listening to excerpts of music	40	35%
Assignment	Composition or arrangement (10 marks) Composing review (5 marks) Analysis (5 marks)	20	15%
Performance – instrument 1 or voice	Live performance marked by a visiting assessor	30	25%

Optional components	How it will be assessed	Marks available	Scaled mark
A choice of — Performance – instrument 2 or voice	Live performance marked by a visiting assessor	30	25%
Or — Portfolio	Submission of compositions and/or arrangements (20 marks) and a composing review (10 marks)	30	25%

The course assessment will provide the basis for the final grade awarded (A, B, C or D). Your final grade will be based on the total percentage for all four course assessment components added together (i.e. the scaled marks for the three mandatory components, plus the scaled mark for your choice of optional component).

DON'T FORGET

You have a choice between performing on two instruments or one instrument and voice, *or* performing on one instrument or voice and submitting a portfolio of compositions and/or arrangements.

QUESTION PAPER OVERVIEW

You will have a final written exam in the form of a question paper. This is based on listening to excerpts of music and answering questions on what you hear, and will last approximately 1 hour and 15 minutes. The question paper is marked out of 40, and will then be scaled to a mark out of 35, meaning that it will be worth 35% of your course award.

The purpose of the question paper is to test your knowledge and understanding of music concepts and music literacy. Different types of questions will be used, requiring you to:

- identify concepts in a range of excerpts of music and styles
- apply music literacy skills
- analyse two excerpts of music, identifying similarities and differences
- identify the style(s) and/or period(s) of two excerpts of music and providing a justification.

All the questions in the question paper are compulsory.

The following sections provide advice on what to revise for the question paper, examples of the types of questions you will come across, and some tips on how to go about answering the questions.

contd

Course assessment: Course overview

TOPICS TO REVISE

The questions in the exam will test your knowledge and understanding of music concepts from styles that you will have covered throughout your course, such as the following:

- Renaissance music (pavan, galliard, ballett, madrigal and ayre)
- Sacred music (Mass, motet, anthem and chorale)
- Twentieth-century music (serial music, tone row / note row, inversion, retrograde, Neoclassical music, polytonality and bitonality)
- Vocal music (ayre, countertenor, song cycle, sprechgesang and bridge)
- Instrumental groups (consort and piano trio)
- Textures (antiphonal, fugue, subject, answer, countersubject and stretto)
- Popular music styles (contemporary jazz and electronic dance music – EDM)

Questions in the Advanced Higher Music paper may also draw on topics that would have been covered at lower levels, such as the following:

- Baroque music (basso continuo, concerto grosso, ritornello, passacaglia, ripieno, ground bass and concertino)
- Classical and Romantic music (sonata, chamber music, string quartet, sonata form, exposition and subject)
- Twentieth-century music styles (minimalist, Impressionist and musique concrète)
- Vocal music (recitative, lied, da capo aria, coloratura and through-composed)
- Sacred music (plainchant, Mass and oratorio)
- Identifying individual instruments and combinations of instruments
- Identifying playing techniques (arco, pizzicato, tremolando and harmonics)
- Popular music styles (jazz funk and soul)
- Scottish music
- World music

Some of the questions will also test your knowledge and understanding of music literacy, including the following:

- Transposing from bass clef into treble clef
- Scales and key signatures
- Chords, cadences, and inversions of chords
- Rhythm/tempo – irregular time signatures, time changes and ties
- Signs, symbols and abbreviations

DON'T FORGET

Revise music concepts and styles from N3, N4, N5 and Higher as well as those introduced at Advanced Higher.

QUESTION STYLES

The questions in the exam will be in a variety of formats, including:

- multiple choice questions, choosing concepts from a range of options
- writing short answers (single words or short phrases)
- following a music guide and inserting appropriate concepts in order
- music literacy (involving music notation and identifying chords)
- identifying prominent concepts in a piece of music under given headings
- comparing two excerpts of music and identifying concepts common to both.

The number of marks available for each question will be indicated at the right-hand side of the page of the question paper.

In the next few sections you will see examples of how these questions will look, along with advice on how to answer them.

ONLINE

Look at examples of Advanced Higher Music past papers by clicking the link on the Digital Zone at www.brightredbooks.net/subjects.

 THINGS TO DO AND THINK ABOUT

Look through some examples of Advanced Higher Music past papers. You will be able to source them online. Even without the audio excerpts of music you can still get a feel for the kinds of questions that are likely to be in the exam, and how they are laid out, which means you'll have a better idea of what to expect.

63

COURSE ASSESSMENT
THE QUESTION PAPER 1

MULTIPLE CHOICE QUESTIONS

Multiple choice questions simply ask you to identify concepts that you hear in the music, chosen from a given list.

There will be different types of multiple choice question, asking you to:
- select **one** correct answer from **four** options
- select **one** correct music literacy answer from **three** options
- select **four** correct answers from **ten** options

Some multiple choice questions will require you to tick (✓) **one** box to identify the correct answer, while others will require you to write your answers on the lines below a list of concepts.

Select one correct answer from four options

This is the most straightforward type of multiple choice question, requiring you to select one correct answer from a choice of four. The question is worth 1 mark.

> Listen to this excerpt and tick (✓) **one** box to identify the harmonic feature that you hear.
> ☐ Suspension
> ☐ Added 6th
> ☐ Tritone
> ☐ Tierce de Picardie

DON'T FORGET

Remember to tick only **one** box for this question.

In this question you are simply required to tick **one** box to identify the appropriate concept. Remember to tick only **one** box.

Here are tips to help you answer this type of question.
- Read over the concepts, trying to anticipate how each might sound.
- If you are not sure of the correct answer, try to eliminate the concepts that are definitely not present. This will help you to narrow your options.

DON'T FORGET

If you tick an incorrect concept by mistake, simply cross out the incorrect answer and tick the correct one. Just make it clear which concept you are choosing.

Select one correct music literacy answer from three options

This type of multiple choice question will require you to follow music notation and select the correct version of the melody from a choice of three. The question is worth 1 mark.

> Listen to this excerpt and tick (✓) **one** box to identify the correct version of the music.
>
> You now have 30 seconds to read through the possible answers.
>
> The excerpt is short and will be played **three** times.
>
> Here is the music for the first time.
> Here is the music for the second time.
> Here is the music for the third time.

In this question you are simply required to tick **one** box to identify the correct version of the music notation. The music notation could be either melodic or rhythmic. Remember to only tick **one** box.

contd

64

Course assessment: The Question Paper 1

Here are some tips to help you answer this type of question.

- Look through the different versions of the notation and try to anticipate how each sounds.
- Look at the shape of the melody (e.g. where it goes up and where it goes down).
- Look at the intervals in the melody (e.g. look out for any noticeable steps or leaps).
- Look out for differences (e.g. where one version has a step where another has a leap, or if one version ascends where the another descends).

Select four correct answers from ten options

This type of multiple choice question will require you to select four correct answers from a choice of ten options. However, you are not required tick the correct answers here. Instead, you are required to write your answers on the lines below. The question is worth 4 marks – 1 mark for each correct answer.

> This question features instrumental music.
>
> Listen to this excerpt and identify **four** concepts in the music from those listed below.
> You now have **15 seconds** to read through the list of features.
>
> | Neoclassical | Basso continuo |
> |---|---|
> | Piano trio | Ritornello |
> | Song cycle | Countertenor |
> | Suspension | Hemiola |
> | Recitative | Ayre |
>
> Insert your **four** answers on the lines below.
> _____
> _____
> _____
> _____
>
> The music will be played **twice** with a pause of 10 seconds between playings and a pause of 40 seconds before the next question starts.
>
> Here is the music for the first time.
> Here is the music for the second time.

DON'T FORGET

For this type of question look carefully at the overall shape of the melody.

DON'T FORGET

Make sure you identify the correct number of concepts, and listen out for concepts that are likely to be related.

DON'T FORGET

If you are not sure of the correct answers, try to eliminate any concepts that are definitely not present. This will help you to narrow your options.

In this type of question, you are required to identify a specified number of concepts from a given list. You should write the correct concepts on the lines below the list. You are not required to write the concepts in a particular order. You just need to identify the four correct concepts.

Here are some tips to help you answer this type of question.

- Read the question carefully to make sure you know how many concepts you are required to identify.
- It can be helpful to consider which concepts might be related (i.e. which combination of concepts are likely to be found in the same piece or style of music). It might also be helpful to consider which concepts are not related (i.e. combinations of concepts that would be unlikely to be found in the same piece or style of music).

DON'T FORGET

If you insert an incorrect answer by mistake, simply cross out the incorrect answer and insert the correct one. Just make it clear which concept you are choosing.

THINGS TO DO AND THINK ABOUT

Create a mind map for each topic or music style that you have studied. This will help you to consider which concepts are related and are likely to be found in the same piece or style of music. It will also help you avoid choosing inappropriate combinations of unrelated concepts that would not be found in the same piece or style of music.

COURSE ASSESSMENT
THE QUESTION PAPER 2

WRITING SHORT ANSWERS (SINGLE WORDS OR SHORT PHRASES)

Some questions will require you to write one or two words or a short phrase. In this type of question, you will not be given a list of concepts to choose from. Instead, you will need to identify the concepts yourself by listening to the music. It is important to note that in this type of question the answer **must** be a concept introduced at either Higher or Advanced Higher level. One mark is available for each answer.

For example, if you are asked to identify an ornament, the answer would need to be an ornament introduced at either Higher or Advanced Higher level. Therefore, the correct answer would have to be **acciaccatura** or **mordent** (Higher concepts) or **appoggiatura** or **turn** (Advanced Higher concepts). Neither grace note nor trill would be acceptable answers, even if these ornaments were present, as they are both N5 concepts.

Or, if you are asked to identify a vocal form, the answer would need to be **da capo aria** or **through-composed** (Higher concepts) or **song cycle** (an Advanced Higher concept). Concepts such as strophic or verse and chorus would not be acceptable answers as they are from N5 and N4 levels.

(a) Listen to the following excerpt and identify a feature of the harmony.
_____

(b) Listen to a continuation of the previous excerpt and identify the ornament.
_____

(c) Listen to this excerpt and identify the type of group playing.
_____

(d) Listen to a new excerpt and identify the style of the music.
_____

(e) Identify the cadence heard at the end of this excerpt.
_____

(f) Listen to another excerpt and identify the type of work.
_____

DON'T FORGET

In questions that require you to write one or two words or a short phrase, the answer must be a Higher or Advanced Higher concept.

DON'T FORGET

In this question, the concepts can be drawn from all levels including N3, N4 and N5, as well as Higher and Advanced Higher.

MUSIC GUIDE

In this type of question, you will be asked to identify features of a piece of music in the order they occur in the excerpt. A guide to the music will be laid out for you to follow. The guide will generally consist of four short statements with areas that are left blank. You will be required to write the correct concepts in these blank areas to complete the statements. There is 1 mark available for each correct answer.

contd

Course assessment: The Question Paper 2

In this question you will hear instrumental music.

In this excerpt you are required to complete the guide below by inserting appropriate music concepts.

There will now be a pause of 30 seconds to allow you to read through the question.

The music will be played **three** times, with a pause of 20 seconds between playings and a pause of 30 seconds before the next question.

In the first two playings a voice will help guide you through the music. There is no voice in the third playing.

Here is the music for the first time.
Here is the music for the second time.
Here is the music for the third time.

1. The melody is played by a/an
   _____

2. The texture is
   _____

3. The rhythmic feature is a/an
   _____

4. The excerpt finishes with a
   _____ cadence.

Here are some tips to help you answer this type of question.

- Read the statements in the guide carefully during the time allowed. The wording will help you focus on possible answers before you even hear the music. For example, if you are asked to identify a rhythmic feature, focus on rhythm concepts. Or, if you are asked to identify a harmonic feature, limit your options to harmony concepts.
- Follow the guide carefully while the music is playing.
- Pay particular attention to where the numbers are read out by the voice during the first and second playings of the music. These numbers will draw your attention to exactly where the concepts will be heard.
- There may be more than one possible answer.

Each answer you provide must be a music concept.

Sometimes the correct answer will be an Italian term or abbreviation.

MUSIC TERMINOLOGY

If there is an Italian term for a particular concept, use the Italian term in preference to the English equivalent. Also, if a particular feature could be described correctly by two different concepts, try to use the highest level concept.

 THINGS TO DO AND THINK ABOUT

Look at the concepts lists for all levels – N3, N4, N5, Higher and Advanced Higher, and consider the following.

- Make sure you know which concepts come under particular headings, for example styles, melody/harmony, rhythm/tempo, texture/structure/form, and timbre.
- Within each heading, consider which concepts appear at different levels, particularly those introduced at Higher and Advanced Higher.

67

COURSE ASSESSMENT
THE QUESTION PAPER 3

MUSIC LITERACY

Questions involving music literacy will require you to answer questions relating to printed music. Some music literacy questions may be quite short, consisting of either a short phrase or just a few bars of music. Other questions might be more extended with several parts, requiring you to identify several features or insert some elements of music notation.

General advice

The following advice is offered for approaching music literacy questions.

- For a short music literacy question, you may only be required to identify one or two features of the music. Focus specifically on what you are being asked to do.
- With a more extended question, you will hear the music more than once. On the first hearing you should listen carefully to the excerpt while you follow the music, and not write anything at this stage. Just familiarise yourself with the music – both how it sounds and what it looks like.
- Remember that some of the notes, rhythms, rests, accidentals, the time signature(s) or the key signature(s) might be missing, as part of the question may require you to insert these.
- You will then be given time to read over the question and see exactly what you are being asked to do. The amount of time given will depend on how many parts there are to that question. The music will then be played again with a pause between playings and a further pause before the next question begins.

DON'T FORGET

Pay close attention to exactly what you are asked to do and take note of how many times you will hear the excerpt.

DON'T FORGET

Pay close attention to how many times the music will be played, and how long the pauses will be between playings and at the end. These can vary slightly depending on the question.

MUSIC LITERACY QUESTION

This question is based on instrumental music *Poco Adagio* by Haydn. Listen and follow the guide to the music below. Here is the music.

You now have time to read through parts (i), (ii), (iii) and (iv).

(i) In the box provided name the key of the excerpt.
(ii) Write the enharmonic equivalent of the boxed note in bar 9.
(iii) Identify the interval between the two boxed notes in bar 11.
(iv) Insert the missing notes in bar 17.

ONLINE

Listen to *Poco Adagio* by clicking the link on the Digital Zone at www.brightredbooks.net/subjects.

The music will be played a specified number of times, with pauses between playings and a further pause before the next question.

You should write all your answers on the guide to the music above.

contd

FURTHER EXAMPLES OF QUESTIONS

Further examples of what you might be asked in a music literacy question.

- Name the key of the music or insert the key signature at the appropriate place.
- Insert the time signature at the appropriate place.
- Identify an interval formed between two notes.
- Insert missing notes – the rhythm will sometimes be printed above or below the stave.
- Identify the type of scale formed by certain notes.
- Insert a missing accidental in front of a particular note.
- Write the enharmonic equivalent of a particular note.
- Insert a missing rest (or rests), a missing tie, or missing barlines.
- Name a chord outlined from the given notes.
- Identify chords, using either letter names or numbers.
- Identify a cadence at a specific place, or insert chords at cadence points.
- Identify 1st and 2nd inversions of major and minor triads in the keys of C, G, F, D and B flat major and A, E and D minor.
- Identify chord II and its 1st inversion in the major keys as listed above.
- Identify chords such as the diminished 7th, dominant 7th, added 6th and the augmented triad.
- Rewrite (in either treble or bass clef) a note at the same pitch.
- Transpose notes from the treble clef one octave lower into bass clef.
- Add or identify signs, symbols or performance directions.
- Create a bass line using chord information provided.

> **DON'T FORGET**
>
> Intervals may include the tritone, augmented 4th and diminished 5th.

> **DON'T FORGET**
>
> Studying the music literacy section of this study guide will help you to revise the music literacy concepts introduced at Advanced Higher.

CREATING A BASS LINE

One of the music literacy questions may require you to create a bass line using chord information provided. The chord information will be provided in two ways:

- guitar chord symbols indicating if the chords are in root position (e.g. D, A, G or Em), first inversion (1st Inv.) or second inversion (2nd Inv.)
- Roman numerals indicating if the chords are in root position (e.g. I, II, IV, V or VI), first inversion (Ib, IIb, IVb, Vb or VIb) or second inversion (Ic, IIc, IVc, Vc or VIc).

The rhythm would also be provided below the stave, as in the following example.

The correct answer for the above example would be as follows. Notice that the bass line is written in the bass clef.

> **ONLINE**
>
> Listen to these examples of music while following the score by clicking the link on the Digital Zone.
> - Minuet in F by Mozart
> - *Sarabande* by Handel
> - Violin sonata in F by Corelli
> - *Siciliano* by Bach
> - Violin sonata by Mozart
> - Oboe sonata by Hindemith
> - Romanian folk dances by Bartók
> - Folk song by Schumann
> - *Ich grolle nicht* by Schumann
> - Blues No. 1 by Christopher Norton
>
> www.brightredbooks.net/subjects.

 ## THINGS TO DO AND THINK ABOUT

Listen to performances of music while following the printed music. Try to listen to piano pieces or instrumental/vocal pieces with a piano accompaniment, paying attention to the bass line as well as the melody.

COURSE ASSESSMENT
SOME HELPFUL TIPS

DON'T FORGET

It is possible for the key signature to change during a piece of music.

DON'T FORGET

It is possible for the time signature to change during a piece of music.

DON'T FORGET

You can revise writing enharmonic equivalents by referring to page 53 in this study guide.

MUSIC LITERACY QUESTIONS

Here are some tips to help you answer different types of music literacy questions.

- When naming the key of the music you will only be expected to identify the keys of C major, G major, F major, D major, B flat major, A minor, E minor and D minor. Make sure you know the key signatures for these keys, and which accidentals you might expect to see if the music is in a minor key.
- The key signature should appear at the start of every stave.
- The time signature should appear only at the beginning of the music, immediately after the key signature. The time signature consists of two numbers, one above the other, and should not be written as a fraction. Make sure that you know the difference between time signatures in simple time and compound time.
- When identifying an interval formed between two notes, always count from the lower note to the higher note.
- When completing missing notes, take care to write notes and rhythms accurately, with the note heads written clearly on the appropriate lines or in the appropriate spaces.
- When inserting a missing accidental, take care to use the correct sign: flat (♭), sharp (#) or natural (♮). Also, remember that any accidental comes immediately before the note head and should be written clearly on the appropriate line or in the appropriate space.
- When writing the enharmonic equivalent of a particular note, remember that you will need to write a note with a different name that sounds the same. For example, D flat (D♭) can be written as C sharp (C#); A sharp (A#) could be written as B flat (B♭).
- When inserting a missing rest, make sure that the bar adds up to the appropriate number of beats. Sometimes you may need to insert more than one rest to make up the correct number of beats. Also, make sure that you know how to group notes and rests in both simple time and compound time.
- When inserting missing ties, remember that notes may be tied across bars.
- When identifying chords, you can use either chord letter names or chord numbers. Chord letter names would be in the form of guitar chord names printed above the stave; for example, in the key of F major, that would be F, B flat, C and Dm (D minor). When using chord numbers, the convention is to use Roman numerals: I, IV, V and VI. Listen carefully to the bass notes (i.e. the lowest notes). This will help you to decide if a chord is in root position or first inversion. Looking carefully at the notes of the melody may also give you a clue as to which chords are used, as melody notes often outline chords.
- When transposing notes from bass clef up one octave into the treble clef, or rewriting (in either treble or bass clef) a note at the same pitch, take care to write the notes accurately on the given blank stave, ensuring that both the pitch and rhythm are correct. Each note must have the majority of note heads in the correct place (i.e. on the correct line or in the correct space) and note heads must be appropriately filled in. Any accidentals must also be correctly placed before the appropriate note.
- Adding signs, symbols or performance directions to the printed music might involve inserting repeat signs, 1st and 2nd time endings, phrase marks, slurs, accents, staccato or dynamic markings, *8va* (octave higher), *8vb* (octave lower), dal segno (D.S.) and *Fine*.
- When identifying where a particular feature occurs in the music, you may be required to annotate the printed music in some way to indicate where you hear a feature. Examples of this might include:

Write [A] above the note where you hear a suspension.
Write [B] above the stave where the bassoon enters.
Write [C] above the note where you hear a turn.
Write [D] above the bar where you hear a plagal cadence.
Write [E] above the note that is harmonised by an augmented triad.

70

Course assessment: Some helpful tips

CREATING A BASS LINE USING CHORD INFORMATION PROVIDED

Here is some guidance to help you answer the music literacy question on creating a bass line.

In creating a bass line, remember that the chord information provided will give you not only the name of the chord, but also the inversion. Knowing the inversion of the chord is an essential factor in deciding which bass notes to use. There will generally be no music played for this type of question as you should be able to work out the bass line from the chord information provided. Remember that the bass line will generally be written using the bass clef.

DON'T FORGET

You can revise chords and their inversions by referring to pages 54 and 55 in this study guide.

SOME GENERAL ADVICE

It will be possible to answer some parts of music literacy questions without actually hearing the music, for example naming the key of the music or inserting a key signature, describing an interval, inserting a missing rest, transposing notes from bass clef up one octave into the treble clef or rewriting (in either treble or bass clef) a note at the same pitch, or writing an enharmonic equivalent.

However, for other parts of the questions – for example those requiring you to insert missing notes, rhythms or accidentals, identify cadences, or identify whereabouts a particular feature occurs in the music – you will need to follow the music very carefully.

During the time that you have to read over the question, you might find it helpful to decide which parts you will be able to answer without hearing the music and which parts can only be answered by following the music. This will help focus your listening on those specific parts of the question where you will need to follow the music. You can then complete the parts of the question that don't require you to hear the music during the time you have at the end.

DON'T FORGET

You will be able to answer some parts of a music literacy question without actually hearing the music.

 THINGS TO DO AND THINK ABOUT

Download some AH Music past papers from the SQA website. When reading over an extended music literacy question, consider which parts of the question you can answer without hearing the music and which parts can only be answered by hearing the music. This will help you to focus on what you actually need to listen for.

You might consider either ticking or crossing off each part of the question as you answer it. This will enable you to easily see which parts of the question you still need to answer.

COURSE ASSESSMENT

IDENTIFYING PROMINENT CONCEPTS AND ANALYSIS 1

This is the most substantial question in the Advanced Higher Music question paper. You will be required first to comment on two excerpts of music, and then to analyse and compare the two excerpts.

The question will be divided into sections (a) and (b) as follows.

Identifying

(a) Listen to each excerpt. For each excerpt identify at least **two** prominent concepts in each of the following categories:
- **Melody/harmony**
- **Rhythm/texture/structure/form/timbre/dynamics**

Both excerpts will be played twice, with a pause of 15 seconds between playings, and with a pause of 4 minutes at the end for you to complete your final answer.

A warning tone will sound 30 seconds before the start of part (b).

You may use the table for rough working, but your final answer must be written on the appropriate page.

Your final answer could be bullet points or short answers identifying the concepts you have heard.

Here is Excerpt 1 for the first time.
Here is Excerpt 2 for the first time.

Here is Excerpt 1 for the second time.
Here is Excerpt 2 for the second time.

You now have 4 minutes to identify at least **four** concepts in each excerpt.

A warning tone will sound **30 seconds** before the start of part (b).

> **DON'T FORGET**
> The specific categories may change slightly from year to year.

ROUGH WORK

Melody/harmony		
Rhythm/texture/ structure/form/ timbre/dynamics		

contd

Course assessment: Identifying prominent concepts and analysis 1

Your final answer must be written on the appropriate page, which will look like this:

FINAL ANSWER

(i) Excerpt 1

_____
_____
_____
_____

(ii) Excerpt 2

_____
_____
_____
_____

There are 2 marks available for each excerpt.

Here are some tips to help you answer this part of the question.

- Listen out for the **most prominent** concepts in each excerpt and don't try to write down everything that you hear.
- Try to identify **at least two** prominent concepts under each of the **two** general categories.
- When writing your final answer, you may choose any of the following approaches:
  o writing your answer in sentences
  o writing concepts as a list, or bullet points
  o listing concepts under the headings provided.

DON'T FORGET

Remember to write your final answer on the page that says FINAL ANSWER.

DON'T FORGET

Make brief notes as you listen in the ROUGH WORK section. Remember that your *rough work* will not be marked. Marks will only be awarded for your final answer.

DON'T FORGET

Try to identify at least **two prominent concepts** under each of the given categories. Avoid writing long lists of contradictory or unrelated concepts.

THINGS TO DO AND THINK ABOUT

Listen to some examples of music and try to identify the most prominent concepts that you hear. Make a list of one or two concepts under each the following headings:

- Style
- Melody/harmony
- Rhythm/tempo
- Texture/structure/form
- Timbre
- Dynamics

Listen for the most prominent concepts and don't try to write down everything you hear.

You should refer to the table of Advanced Higher concepts on page 5 of this study guide, as well as the tables of concepts from other levels (N3, N4, N5, and Higher), to remind yourself which concepts come under the different headings.

COURSE ASSESSMENT

IDENTIFYING PROMINENT CONCEPTS AND ANALYSIS 2

Analysis and Conclusion

The second part of this question requires you to analyse the two excerpts of music you have been listening to, and to provide an extended answer comparing the two excerpts.

This part of the question will be divided into two parts, (i) and (ii), as follows.

> (b) This question has two parts.
> (i) **Analyse** the **two** excerpts you have just heard.
> In your extended answer you should refer to **six similarities/differences** across the following categories:
> - **Type of work**
> - **Melody/harmony**
> - **Rhythm/texture/structure/form/timbre/dynamics**
> (ii) **Conclude** your analysis with a statement on the **style/period** of each excerpt and **justify** your answer.
>
> You will hear each excerpt **two** more times, with a pause of 15 seconds between playings, and a further **10 minutes** to complete your answers for part (i) and part (ii).
>
> **Rough work will not be marked.**
>
> You should write your final answers on the appropriate pages.
>
> Here is Excerpt 1 for the third time.
> Here is Excerpt 2 for the third time.
>
> Here is Excerpt 1 for the last time.
> Here is Excerpt 2 for the last time.
>
> You now have **10 minutes** to complete your analysis and conclusion.
>
> A warning tone will sound 30 seconds before the end of the question paper.

DON'T FORGET

Rough work will not be marked. This is only for you to make notes to prepare your final answer.

ROUGH WORK

_____
_____
_____
_____
_____
_____
_____
_____
_____

Course assessment: Identifying prominent concepts and analysis 2

FINAL ANSWER

(i) Analysis
Comment on **six similarities/differences** you hear in the excerpts. Your final answer should be a written description of what you have heard and not simply a list of similarities/differences.

_____
_____
_____
_____
_____

(ii) Conclusion
Write a statement on the **style/period** of each excerpt and **justify** your answer.

_____
_____
_____

There are 4 marks available for part (i) Analysis and 2 marks available for part (ii) Conclusion.

DON'T FORGET

Your final answer must be written as a series of statements clearly identifying similarities and differences, and not just a list of similarities and differences.

SOME HELPFUL TIPS

Here are some tips to help you answer this question.

- Make sure the concepts you identify are relevant to the categories stated in the question.
- Focus on the most prominent concepts and avoid writing long lists of unrelated concepts.
- Give all the relevant information to show that you understand the music.
- Justify your answer to 6(b)(ii), using evidence from earlier parts of the question, to provide an answer that clearly identifies the features relating to the style or period of the music.
- Focus on providing the period of music for each excerpt before giving a justification that specifically identifies the features in each excerpt that are characteristic of the period.
- Listen particularly to the harmonic features of the music when deciding on a period.
- Listen to the excerpt as a whole before deciding on the period, as some features may be common to more than one period.

DON'T FORGET

You must write your final answers in the appropriate places as rough work will _not_ be marked.

DON'T FORGET

Remember to identify the type of work in your answer to question 6(b)(i).

THINGS TO DO AND THINK ABOUT

Listen to a wide range of music from different styles and periods, considering which musical features are particularly characteristic of each period or style. Create a short list of features associated with different musical periods and styles, remembering that some features may appear in more than one style or period. Try to focus on features that are unique to a particular style or period.

ASSIGNMENT

OVERVIEW AND COMPOSING REVIEW

STRUCTURE OF THE ASSIGNMENT

The assignment is a mandatory component of the course assessment and has three parts:

- composing or arranging one piece of music
- reviewing the creative process of your composition or arrangement
- analysing a chosen piece of music.

The assignment is worth 20 marks out of a total of 120, which are awarded as follows:

- composing or arranging music (10 marks)
- review of the creative process (5 marks)
- analysis (5 marks).

The mark out of 20 is then scaled to represent 15% of the course assessment.

The following sections provide an overview of what is required for each part of the assignment.

COMPOSING OR ARRANGING MUSIC

The piece of music that you compose or arrange can be in any style or genre that you choose. It must be no shorter than 1 minute and no longer than 4½ minutes.

If your composition or arrangement is longer than 4½ minutes, you may need to consider either cutting some of the music or fading out to keep within the time limit.

DON'T FORGET

Your composition or arrangement should be no shorter than 1 minute and no longer than 4½ minutes.

For a composition you must:

- plan your composition
- explore and develop musical ideas using all the musical elements of melody, harmony, rhythm, structure and timbre
- create one complete piece of music.

For an arrangement you must:

DON'T FORGET

An arrangement must be a creative reworking of your chosen piece of music, and not just a transcription of the original.

- plan your arrangement
- creatively rework the chosen music by exploring and developing musical ideas using all the musical elements of melody, harmony, rhythm, structure and timbre
- create one arrangement.

If you submit an arrangement, you must also include a copy of the original sheet music for the piece or song you have arranged. You must also make clear your own input in the review of the creative process by providing details of what you have done to make the arrangement different from the original music.

REVIEW OF THE CREATIVE PROCESS

In reviewing the creative process of your composition or arrangement, you must refer to the compositional methods used and clearly show how you have explored and developed musical ideas using all the elements of melody, harmony, rhythm, structure and timbre. Your review must include clear details of:

DON'T FORGET

Your composition or arrangement must use all the elements of melody, harmony, rhythm, structure and timbre.

- the main decisions you have made
- how you have explored and developed musical ideas
- strengths and/or areas for improvement.

76

Assignment: Overview and composing review

ANALYSIS

As well as submitting a composition or arrangement and a review of the creative process, you must also choose a piece of music and analyse the key features with reference to compositional methods and music concepts. You cannot analyse your own music in this part of the assignment. Your analysis must contain reference to at least five of the following musical elements:
- style
- melody
- harmony
- rhythm and tempo
- texture
- structure and/or form
- timbre and dynamics.

You must also provide an audio recording of the music you have chosen to analyse. This could be in the form of either an audio file or a weblink to an online source. Your analysis must include audio time codes referencing the key features you identify. It is not necessary to provide edited excerpts of the audio recording. You may also include sections of a score or a guide to the music referencing the key features you have identified.

 DON'T FORGET

You must provide an audio recording of the piece of music or song you have chosen to analyse.

EVIDENCE TO BE SUBMITTED FOR THE ASSIGNMENT

There are specific pieces of evidence that you need to submit for each part of the assignment.

For composing you must submit the following three pieces of evidence:
- an audio recording of your composition
- a score or performance plan of your composition
- a review of your creative process detailing how you have explored and developed musical ideas using the musical elements of melody, harmony, rhythm, structure and timbre.

For arranging you must submit the following four pieces of evidence:
- an audio recording of your arrangement
- a score or performance plan of your arrangement
- a copy of the original sheet music for the piece or song you have arranged
- a review of your creative process detailing how you have explored and developed musical ideas using the musical elements of melody, harmony, rhythm, structure and timbre.

For the analysis you must submit the following two pieces of evidence:
- an analysis of your chosen piece of music, including references to time codes
- an audio recording of the piece of music you have chosen to analyse, either as an audio file or as a weblink to an online source.

The review for your composing or arranging can be presented either in continuous prose or as bullet points and should be approximately 200–350 words long.

The analysis of your chosen piece of music should be presented in prose as clear statements, showing an understanding of the key musical features, and should be approximately 600–800 words long.

The suggested word counts are intended to indicate the volume of evidence required. No penalty will be applied for submissions that are below or above the word count. However, you should try to avoid submitting something so short that it contains very little information, or something that is so long that it contains either irrelevant or too much unnecessary detail.

You must use the SQA review of the creative process and analysis templates, which are available on the SQA Advanced Higher Music subject page. You can also download draft templates, with guidance notes, from the Bright Red Digital Zone.

 **ONLINE**

Download draft review and analysis templates, with guidance notes, from www.brightredbooks.net/subjects.

DON'T FORGET

Check exactly what evidence you are required to submit for each part of the assignment.

 THINGS TO DO AND THINK ABOUT

In preparation for the assignment, you should:
- decide whether you would like to work with composing or arranging, or experiment with both
- think about how you will keep a record of your progress
- consider whether you will create either a score or a performance plan for your composition or arrangement
- start listening to some pieces of music that you might consider analysing.

ASSIGNMENT

COMPOSING

There are many different approaches to composing music. The advice offered here is intended to provide some suggestions as to how you might approach the composing element of the assignment. Much of the advice about how you might work with compositional methods can be applied equally well to both composing and arranging.

WHERE TO START?

You have the freedom to compose a piece of music in any style or genre, although you may wish to work within a style or genre that particularly interests you, or that you are already familiar with.

Some possible starting points for you to consider are given below.

If you play an instrument such as the piano, keyboard or guitar, you might decide to compose a piece of music for:
- your chosen instrument
- your chosen instrument along with another instrument
- your chosen instrument within an ensemble.

If you play an orchestral instrument, you might decide to compose a piece of music for:
- your chosen instrument along with an accompanying instrument
- a suitable ensemble that includes your chosen instrument, such as a woodwind group, brass band, wind band, string quartet or string ensemble.

If you are a singer, or are interested in song writing, you might decide to compose:
- a song with instrumental accompaniment (e.g. piano or guitar)
- a song for a band or a group
- music for a vocal ensemble or choir.

If you are interested in music technology, you might decide to compose music using:
- multi-track recording techniques
- computer programmes for recording music or creating scores
- apps that enable you to create your own backing tracks or manipulate sounds.

DON'T FORGET

Make sure that you are aware of the range and technical capabilities of any instrument(s) you compose for.

DON'T FORGET

Some orchestral instruments need to have music written in different clefs or transposed into different keys.

DON'T FORGET

Make sure that you know the range and combination of voices you have available.

DON'T FORGET

If you use pre-recorded loops or samples, this must be done within the context of a wider composition and clearly show your own creative input.

MELODY

In creating a melody, you might begin with simple ideas that could be developed using techniques such as repetition or sequences. To add some more sophistication to your melody you could experiment with:
- modes – creating a melody using a particular mode
- adding ornaments – acciaccaturas, appoggiaturas, turns or mordents
- different scales – harmonic minor, melodic minor or whole-tone
- modulation to different keys – such as the relative minor or relative major
- serial techniques such as tone row / note row
- intervals such as the tritone, augmented 4th or diminished 5th.

HARMONY

As well as using major and minor chords, you could experiment with:
- different types of chords – e.g. the added 6th, dominant 7th, diminished, diminished 7th, tritone or augmented triad
- different inversions of chords
- different cadences – e.g. a plagal cadence or an interrupted cadence
- modulation to different keys – e.g. relative minor or relative major
- other harmonic devices – such as tierce de Picardie, cluster, suspension, polytonality or bitonality.

Assignment: Composing

RHYTHM/TEMPO

You might decide to use time signatures in simple time or compound time, or features such as syncopation, dotted rhythms or rubato. However, you could also experiment with:
- irregular time signatures – e.g. 5/4
- time changes – alternating between different time signatures
- different rhythmic groupings – e.g. triplets, 3 against 2 or cross rhythms
- other rhythmic devices – e.g. augmentation, diminution, ties or hemiola
- varying the tempo between sections.

TIMBRE

Your exploration of timbre will depend on which combination of instruments or voices you are composing for, or which sounds you are using. If you are composing for a string instrument you might use playing techniques such as arco, pizzicato or con sordino. A composition involving electric guitars may include effects such as reverb or distortion. Any composition could be enhanced by using varied dynamics or even a contrast between legato and staccato. However, you could also experiment with:
- playing techniques – e.g. tremolando or harmonics
- vocal techniques – e.g. a cappella or sprechgesang
- expression markings – e.g. accents, slurs or staccato
- electronic effects – e.g. distortion, reverb, pre-recorded loops, samples or musique concrète techniques.

DON'T FORGET

Your composition must use all the elements of melody, harmony, rhythm, structure and timbre.

TEXTURE/STRUCTURE/FORM

In experimenting with different structures, there is a wide range of forms and textures that you might wish to explore. These include:
- instrumental forms – e.g. binary (AB), ternary (ABA), rondo (ABACA) or theme and variations
- vocal forms – e.g. verse and chorus, strophic or through-composed
- different textures – e.g. contrapuntal/polyphonic, homophonic, fugue or antiphonal
- other structural devices – e.g. inversion, retrograde, subject, answer, countersubject or stretto.

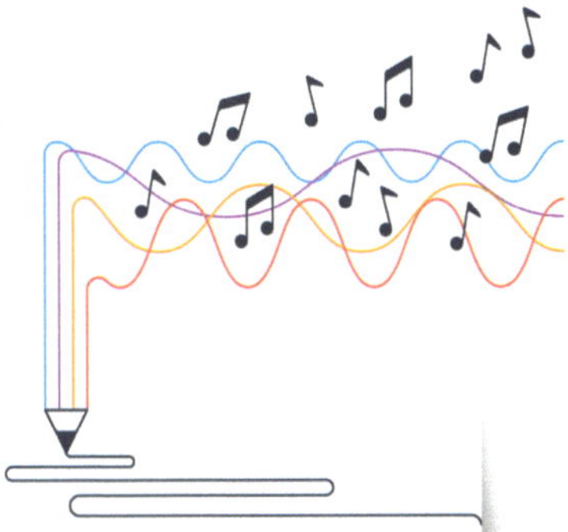

IDEAS

Drawing on sources of inspiration outwith music might include composing:
- music to convey a story or a poem
- a song, using the words of a poem for the lyrics
- music based on a painting or a series of pictures
- music inspired by a particular event.

You could also consider contexts that require music to be composed, and set yourself the task of composing:
- music for a short film or television programme
- music for a video game or incidental music for a play
- music for a special occasion such as a concert or a religious service.

DON'T FORGET

Whatever you choose as the inspiration or context for your composition, try to make your music interesting and imaginative. Take care to structure your musical ideas in an organised way, so that your composition is coherent and musically convincing.

THINGS TO DO AND THINK ABOUT

- Compose for instrument(s) or voice(s) that you are familiar with.
- Keep a record of how you explore and experiment with your musical ideas.
- Reflect on your composing, considering which of your musical ideas are most effective.
- Consider how you will create a score or a performance plan for your composition.
- Decide how you will make an audio recording of your composition.

ASSIGNMENT
ARRANGING

Arranging music involves adapting an existing piece of music or song by using compositional methods to create something that sounds different. Much of the advice in the Composing section about how you might use the elements of melody, harmony, rhythm, structure and timbre, will apply equally well to arranging.

WHERE TO START?

The first thing to keep in mind is that arranging music means reworking a piece of music into something that sounds different from the original. Simply copying the elements of the original piece of music (such as the melody, harmony, rhythm or bass line) and allocating them to different instruments or voices would be a transcription and not an arrangement.

If you arrange a well-known piece of music such as a pop song, Classical piece or film theme, for example, you must avoid re-creating the sound of the original. If your arrangement sounds too much like the original, it will be regarded as a transcription rather than an arrangement.

The following sections offer advice on how you might develop the different elements of the music within arranging.

DON'T FORGET

An arrangement must be a creative reworking of your chosen piece of music and not just a transcription of the original.

MELODY

In developing elements of the melody, you might consider:
- altering the original melody or using fragments of the original melody as motifs
- adding melodic features such as ornaments, a countermelody, or a descant
- repeating part of the original melody using sequences.

DON'T FORGET

Arranging a simple piece of music such as a folk song or traditional tune might be easier, as you will have more scope to make the music sound different.

HARMONY

In developing elements of the harmony, you might consider:
- changing some of the chords or using different types of chords
- using different inversions of chords
- exploring other harmonic devices such as suspensions or modulations.

RHYTHM

In developing elements of the rhythm, you might consider:
- altering the original rhythm, rhythmic style or tempo
- changing the time signature or using an irregular time signature
- exploring other rhythmic devices such as augmentation, diminution, syncopation or hemiola.

TIMBRE

In developing elements of the timbre, you might consider:
- which combination of instruments or voices to use
- performing techniques associated with particular instruments or voices
- playing techniques – e.g. arco, pizzicato or glissando
- adding expression markings or effects.

DON'T FORGET

Make sure that you are aware of the range and technical capabilities of any instrument(s) you use in your arrangement.

80

Assignment: Arranging

STRUCTURE

In developing elements of the structure, you might consider:
- adding new sections such as an introduction, coda, bridge or middle 8
- experimenting with different textures – e.g. contrapuntal/polyphonic, homophonic or antiphonal
- exploring other structural devices such as inversion, retrograde, imitation or ostinato.

STYLE

In developing elements of the style, you might consider reworking a piece of music in a different style, such as:
- arranging a Classical piece in a pop or rock style
- arranging a traditional melody in a jazz or Latin American style
- arranging a popular song in a Baroque or Classical style.

ACTIVITY:

Listen to different examples of arrangements to consider what works well.

INSTRUMENTATION/ORCHESTRATION

Gnomus (*The Gnome*), from Mussorgsky's *Pictures at an Exhibition* is based on a sketch of an awkward and menacing creature who shuffles along, letting out wild shrieks. The original piano piece is very dramatic, making use of wide leaps, discords, changing time signatures, changes in tempo, sforzando chords, and sudden changes in dynamics.

Stokowski's arrangement for orchestra, features prominent use of strings, muted brass, and the xylophone. While it makes use of varied playing techniques, the music is really a transcription of the notes from the original piano solo with very little reworking of the original musical material.

In Ravel's arrangement, the original piano music is also transcribed into an orchestral version. However, Ravel adds new sounds and effects not suggested in the original piano music, such as glissandos in the strings, percussion effects such as a *whip* sound, *rattle*, and the celesta, as well as muted brass. It ends with a crash on the cymbals and the bass drum.

1970s Rock band Emerson, Lake & Palmer recorded a version of *Gnomus* featuring drum kit, bass guitar, electric organ, and synthesizer sounds, and includes improvisation and variations on Mussorgsky's original melody.

ARRANGING IN DIFFERENT STYLES

The original recording of *She Loves You* by The Beatles is in a pop style and features lead vocal, backing vocals, guitars, bass guitar and drum kit.

A jazz-style arrangement of *She Loves You* performed by the Count Basie Orchestra features piano, muted brass, saxophones, drum kit and a walking bass, as well as syncopation and an improvised saxophone solo.

A Baroque-style arrangement of *She Loves You* performed by the Peter Breiner Chamber Orchestra features melodic decoration, countermelodies and sequences, and is performed by strings and harpsichord.

THINGS TO DO AND THINK ABOUT

- Arrange music for instrument(s) or voice(s) that you are familiar with.
- Keep a record of how you explore and experiment with your musical ideas.
- Reflect on your arranging, considering which of your musical ideas are most effective.
- Consider how you will create a score or a performance plan for your arrangement.
- Decide how you will make an audio recording of your arrangement.

DON'T FORGET

Your arrangement must use all the elements of melody, harmony, rhythm, structure and timbre.

ONLINE

Listen to *Gnomus* for solo piano by clicking the link on the Digital Zone at www.brightredbooks.net/subjects.

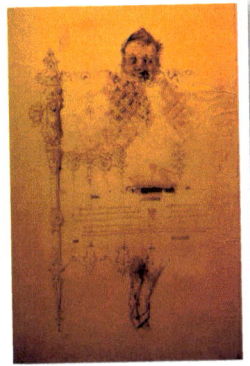

ONLINE

Listen to the different arrangements of *Gnomus* by clicking the link on the Digital Zone at www.brightredbooks.net/subjects.

ONLINE

Listen to *She Loves You* by The Beatles by clicking the link on the Digital Zone at www.brightredbooks.net/subjects.

ONLINE

Listen to the different arrangements of *She Loves You* by clicking the link on the Digital Zone at www.brightredbooks.net/subjects.

ASSIGNMENT
THE COMPOSING OR ARRANGING PROCESS

The advice offered here is designed to help you focus on the process involved in composing or arranging music, and to highlight the various stages you should be aware of. Whether you are composing or arranging music for the assignment or the portfolio option, the process is likely to be the same.

OVERVIEW

The purpose of the composing or arranging music component is to provide you with opportunities to explore and develop musical ideas and compositional methods to create music. The composing/arranging element of the assignment has two parts:
- composing or arranging one piece of music
- reviewing the creative process.

Your composition or arrangement may be in any style or genre and must last a minimum of 1 minute and a maximum of 4½ minutes. The submission of the composing/arranging element of the assignment must include the following:
- an audio recording of your composition or arrangement
- a score or performance plan of your composition or arrangement
- a review of the creative process.

The review of the creative process should demonstrate that you have:
- planned and reviewed your own creative process
- explored and developed musical ideas using appropriate compositional methods
- created one complete piece of music.

In creating your composition or arrangement, it is important to note the following.
- It may contain sections of improvisation, but this must be in the context of a wider composition or arrangement which demonstrates compositional skills. A piece of music which is solely an improvisation is not acceptable.
- If you choose to work with pre-recorded loops or samples this must also be done within the context of a wider composition or arrangement and show the compositional process. Your own creative input must be clearly identifiable.

COMPOSING/ARRANGING TASK

For the composing/arranging element of the assignment, you are required to:
- plan your composition or arrangement
- explore and develop musical ideas using all the elements of melody, harmony, rhythm, timbre and structure
- create one complete piece of music.

During the process of working on your composition or arrangement, you are encouraged to plan, explore, develop and create.

PLAN

In planning your composition or arrangement, you should consider the following.
- What kind of music would you like to create?
- Do you want to compose or arrange music within a particular style or genre that interests you, or do you want to experiment with music in different styles or genres?
- Which instruments or voices you would like to use?
- Will you use a particular structure such as ternary, rondo, verse and chorus, or theme and variations?
- How will you keep a record of the decisions that you make?

DON'T FORGET

Check exactly what you need to submit for the composing or arranging element of the assignment.

Assignment: The Composing or Arranging Process

EXPLORE

In exploring ideas for your composition or arrangement, you should:

- start with simple ideas – you can develop or add to them later
- experiment with musical ideas using all the musical elements of melody, harmony, rhythm, timbre and structure
- experiment with different chords and their inversions
- reflect on your creative process, considering which of your musical ideas are most effective
- keep a record of how you have explored and experimented with musical ideas.

DEVELOP

In developing ideas for your composition or arrangement, you might:

- change some of the musical ideas you have been exploring and experimenting with
- discard some ideas that you feel are not working so well
- extend some of your musical ideas to make your composition or arrangement more imaginative
- incorporate more concepts or musical features into your composition or arrangement to make it more interesting
- keep a record of the ways in which you have explored and developed your musical ideas.

 DON'T FORGET

Keep a record of the main decisions that you make so that you can come back to that when writing your review of the creative process.

CREATE

In creating your final composition or arrangement, you should:

- decide which of your musical ideas work best
- use your best musical ideas to create your composition or arrangement
- remember that your composition or arrangement must include all the musical elements of melody, harmony, rhythm, timbre and structure
- create a score or a performance plan for your composition or arrangement
- create an audio recording of your composition or arrangement
- identify the strengths of your composition or arrangement and consider any areas which may be improved.

It would be helpful to maintain a diary or log to keep a record of the main decisions that you make while working on your composition or arrangement. You can then come back to that when writing your review of the creative process. You must use the SQA review of the creative process template, which is available on the SQA Advanced Higher Music subject page. You can also download draft templates, with guidance notes, from the Bright Red Digital Zone.

ONLINE

Download the draft review of the creative process templates, with guidance notes, from www.brightredbooks.net/subjects.

 THINGS TO DO AND THINK ABOUT

- Compose or arrange music for instrument(s) and/or voice(s) that you are familiar with. This means that the music you create is more likely to be appropriate to the instrument(s) and/or voice(s).
- Experiment with composing or arranging music in different styles or genres. Alternatively, you might decide to work within a style or genre that you particularly enjoy.
- Explore the use of different concepts or compositional methods. Try to use or combine concepts in interesting and imaginative ways.
- Remember to use your musical ideas in an organised way, so that your composition or arrangement is coherent and musically convincing.

ASSIGNMENT
ASSESSMENT OF COMPOSING

This section outlines what the characteristics of a good composition might be. It also provides details of the assessment criteria that will be used to award your composition a mark out of 10.

WHAT A GOOD COMPOSITION LOOKS LIKE

Your composition must use all the musical elements of melody, harmony, rhythm, structure and timbre. The following table provides some examples of what a good composition might include within each of these elements, as well as some common faults that you should try to avoid.

Musical element	What a good composition might include	Some common faults to be avoided
Melody	A good melodic shape, with a variety of steps and leaps	A repetitive or disjointed melody
	Use of ornaments, such as acciaccaturas, appoggiaturas, turns or mordents, as appropriate, to enhance and develop the melody	No melodic decoration or development
	An understanding of scales such as harmonic minor, melodic minor or whole-tone, or the use of modes	Little understanding of scales, scale patterns or modes
	Addition of a countermelody, descant or obbligato to add melodic interest	Little evidence of melodic devices being used
	Different melodic devices such as tone row / note row, or exploring different intervals such as the tritone, augmented 4th or diminished 5th	A limited range of melodic devices explored, or overuse of a particular melodic device
Harmony	A variety of chords, including the added 6th, dominant 7th, diminished, diminished 7th, tritone and augmented triad	A limited range of chords
	A chord progression that is interesting and imaginative	Inappropriate combination of chords
	Different inversions of chords	Chords in root position only
	Modulation from a major key to the relative minor or from a minor key to the relative major	Little variety of keys or little understanding of modulation
	Using cadences, such as a plagal or interrupted, in an appropriate and musically convincing way	Showing little understanding of cadences
Rhythm	Rhythmic variety including rhythms and rhythmic grouping such as triplets, 3 against 2, or cross rhythms	Limited use of rhythms and little rhythmic variety
	Irregular time signatures, such as 5/4, time signatures in compound time, or time changes	Keeping to the same time signature with little rhythmic interest or variety
	Rhythmic devices such as augmentation, diminution, ties, syncopation or hemiola	A limited range of rhythmic devices or overuse of a particular rhythmic device

contd

84

Assignment: Assessment of Composing

Timbre	A variety of instruments or combining instrumental sounds in imaginative ways	One instrument only, with little variety in tone or dynamics
	For a single instrument, making full use of the range and capabilities of the instrument	For a single instrument, making limited use of the range and capabilities of the instrument
	A variety of playing techniques as appropriate to different instruments, e.g. arco, pizzicato, con sordino, tremolando or harmonics	A limited range of playing techniques, or not exploring the playing techniques possible on a particular instrument
	Using slurs, accents or staccato marks to add interest to articulation in the music	Little or no variety in articulation
Structure	Well organised, with musical ideas used in a systematic and musically convincing way	Musical ideas used in a disjointed way or with little sense of organisation
	A clear structure such as ternary form, rondo form, verse and chorus, theme and variations, passacaglia or sonata form	Having little sense of structure
	A range of structural devices appropriate to the style such as inversion, retrograde, subject, answer, countersubject or stretto	A limited range of structural devices or not using them in an appropriate or musically convincing way
	Structural features such as exposition, subject or coda	A limited range of structural features, displaying little contrast
	Contrasting textures such as contrapuntal/polyphonic, homophonic, fugue and antiphonal	Little contrast or limited use of different textures
	Using phrase marks to indicate an understanding of structure	No indication or understanding of phrases

Your composition must include all five elements of melody, harmony, rhythm, timbre and structure.

MARKING CRITERIA

Your composition will be awarded a mark out of 10, based on a range of summary statements. The following table shows a breakdown of the mark range from 0 to 10, along with the related composing music summary statements that will be used to assess your composition.

Mark range	Composing music summary statements
9–10	An excellent composition demonstrating a range of musical ideas that have been developed imaginatively and convincingly, appropriate to the candidate's chosen style. The use of elements is highly creative and effective.
7–8	A good composition demonstrating a range of musical ideas that have been developed with some imagination, appropriate to the candidate's chosen style. The use of elements shows creativity.
5–6	A composition demonstrating musical ideas that have been developed satisfactorily, appropriate to the candidate's chosen style. The use of elements may be simplistic and straightforward.
3–4	A composition demonstrating musical ideas that have been developed inconsistently within the candidate's chosen style. The use of elements is not always appropriate.
1–2	A composition demonstrating limited musical ideas with little or no development within the candidate's chosen style. The use of elements is poor.
0	No evidence produced

You must use all five elements of melody, harmony, rhythm, timbre and structure to gain the full range of marks.

THINGS TO DO AND THINK ABOUT

When reflecting on your own composition, consider the following.
- Have you used all five elements of melody, harmony, rhythm, timbre and structure in your composition?
- Have you explored and developed all of these elements in creative and imaginative ways?
- Have you explored and developed some of these musical elements more than others?
- Referring to the composing music summary statements, which mark range do you think is most applicable to your own composition?
- Could you explore and develop any of the musical elements further to improve your composition?

ASSIGNMENT
ASSESSMENT OF ARRANGING

This section outlines the characteristics of what a good arrangement might be. It also provides details of the assessment criteria that will be used to award your arrangement a mark out of 10. If you choose to submit an arrangement, rather than a composition, you must creatively rework your chosen piece of music by exploring and developing musical ideas using all of the musical elements of melody, harmony, rhythm, structure and timbre.

WHAT A GOOD ARRANGEMENT LOOKS LIKE

Your arrangement must use all the musical elements of melody, harmony, rhythm, structure and timbre. The following table provides some examples of what a good arrangement might include within each of these elements, as well as some common faults that you should try to avoid.

Musical element	What a good arrangement might include	Some common faults to be avoided
Melody	Using fragments from the original melody to create motifs	Copying the original melody without any development
	Adding ornaments as appropriate to enhance and develop the melody	No melodic decoration or development
	Creating a countermelody, descant or obbligato to add interest	Little evidence of a countermelody, descant or obbligato
	Melodic devices such as question and answer, sequence, drone, pedal, inverted pedal or glissando	A limited range of melodic devices, or overuse of a particular melodic device
Harmony	Addition of chords, possibly including the dominant 7th, diminished 7th or added 6th	Keeping only to the same chords as in the original music
	Introducing broken chord or arpeggio patterns to add interest	Keeping only to the same chord figurations from the original music
	Use of modulation, e.g. from a major key to the relative minor or from a minor key to the relative major	No use of modulation
	Changing tonality	Staying with the same tonality as the original music
Rhythm	Varying the rhythm or rhythmic style	Keeping to the original rhythm or rhythmic style
	Varying the tempo	Keeping to the original tempo
	Changing the time signature or using irregular time signatures	Keeping to the original time signature throughout
	Using different rhythmic devices such as augmentation or diminution	Using only rhythmic devices from the original music

DON'T FORGET

If you submit an arrangement, you must also include a copy of the original sheet music for the piece or song you have arranged.

contd

Assignment: Assessment of Arranging

Timbre	Changing instruments or voices from the original music	Using the same instruments or voices from the original music
	Incorporating playing techniques as appropriate to different instruments, e.g. arco and pizzicato strings, finger-picking and strumming the guitar, or using effects such as reverb or distortion	Using a limited range of playing techniques, or not exploring the playing techniques possible on a particular instrument
	Varying the register to add interest	Keeping everything to the same register
Structure	Adding structural features such as introduction, bridge or coda	Keeping to the same structure as the original music
	Developing the music by using contrasting homophonic, polyphonic or contrapuntal textures	Keeping to the same texture as the original music
Style	Changing the style of the music, e.g. • reworking a traditional tune in a jazz style • reworking a pop song in a Baroque or Classical style • reworking a Classical piece in a pop or Latin American style	Keeping the music within the same style

DON'T FORGET

Your arrangement must creatively rework the chosen music by exploring and developing musical ideas using all of the musical elements of melody, harmony, rhythm, structure and timbre.

MARKING CRITERIA

Your arrangement will be awarded a mark out of 10, based on a range of summary statements. The following table shows a breakdown of the mark range from 0 to 10, along with the related arranging music summary statements that will be used to assess your arrangement.

Mark range	Arranging music summary statements
9–10	An excellent arrangement that uses a range of compositional methods to develop aspects of the original piece imaginatively and convincingly. The arrangement skilfully and effectively employs varied instrumental forces and combinations, shows originality, and is highly creative.
7–8	A good arrangement that uses a range of compositional methods to develop aspects of the original piece with some imagination. The arrangement successfully employs varied instrumental forces and combinations, shows some originality, and is creative.
5–6	A satisfactory arrangement that uses compositional methods to show some development of aspects of the original piece. The arrangement employs instrumental forces and combinations in a straightforward way.
3–4	A simplistic arrangement that uses compositional methods to show limited development of aspects of the original piece. Instrumental forces and combinations are not always appropriate.
1–2	A poor arrangement that shows very limited development of aspects of the original piece. Instrumental forces and combinations are inappropriate.
0	No evidence produced

DON'T FORGET

An arrangement cannot be a basic transcription from an available score. You must creatively rework your chosen piece of music.

THINGS TO DO AND THINK ABOUT

When reflecting on your own arrangement, consider the following.
- Have you used all five elements of melody, harmony, rhythm, timbre and structure in your arrangement?
- Have you explored and developed all of these elements in creative and imaginative ways?
- Have you explored and developed some of these musical elements more than others?
- Have you reworked your chosen piece of music using compositional methods and not simply transcribed the original music?
- Referring to the arranging music summary statements, which mark range do you think is most applicable to your own arrangement?
- Could you explore and develop any of these musical elements further to improve your arrangement?

ASSIGNMENT

SCORE OR PERFORMANCE PLAN

Whether you decide to compose or arrange music for your assignment, you will be required to submit a score or a performance plan for your composition or arrangement.

CREATING A SCORE

Creating a score would involve using your knowledge of music literacy to notate the appropriate notes and rhythms for your composition or arrangement. This could be either handwritten or printed using any music notation software.

A score should include all the information required for someone else to be able perform or follow your composition or arrangement. This would include:
- identifying any instrument(s) or voice(s) used
- notes written clearly on the stave or staves
- accurate indication of note values, rhythms and rhythmic groupings
- key signature(s) as appropriate
- time signature(s) as appropriate
- bars and bar lines
- tempo indications
- dynamic markings as appropriate
- appropriate signs and symbols such as repeat signs or first and second time endings
- performance directions relevant to the instrument(s) or voice(s) used, such as arco, pizzicato, con sordino, a cappella or phrase marks
- any other appropriate performance directions, such as slurs, accents or staccato markings.

If you are composing or arranging music for different instruments, it is important to remember that some instruments play from different clefs. In general, higher pitched instruments (such as the flute, oboe, clarinet, trumpet, French horn, violin, saxophone and guitar) play from the treble clef, while lower pitched instruments (such as the bassoon, trombone, tuba, cello, double bass and bass guitar) play from the bass clef. It is also important to note that instruments such as the clarinet, trumpet and various types of saxophones are known as *transposing instruments*, which means that the written music for these instruments will need to be transposed into different keys. Therefore, you will need to find out which clefs and keys are required for certain instruments.

CREATING A PERFORMANCE PLAN

In some styles or genres of music, it may not be appropriate to produce a conventional score that uses standard music notation. This might be the case if your composition or arrangement uses elements of improvisation, is computer based, or uses elements of electronic music or musique concrète. In such cases you may decide to create a performance plan instead. A performance plan is a visual representation of your music that clearly indicates what is happening in the music. Although a performance plan may not include conventional music notation, it still needs to act as a guide to the music. This means that your performance plan would need to clearly identify:
- the overall structure of the music
- any instrument(s) or voice(s) used
- playing or performing techniques used by any instrument(s) or voice(s)
- music concepts or other techniques used in the music
- how the concepts are used or combined
- any effects used, including electronic or digital effects
- any other features relevant to the music.

contd

DON'T FORGET

The score for your composition or arrangement must contain all the information required for someone else to perform or interpret your music.

DON'T FORGET

You must create a score or performance plan for your composition or arrangement, as well as an audio recording.

ONLINE

You can download various manuscript paper templates from the Digital Zone at www.brightredbooks.net/subjects.

DON'T FORGET

The performance plan for your composition or arrangement needs to contain all the information required for someone else to be able to follow what is happening in the music.

88

Assignment: Score or Performance plan

In identifying the overall structure of the music, you may refer to sections of your composition or arrangement using heading such as:

- Introduction
- Verse 1 / Section A
- Chorus / Section B
- Middle 8 / Section C
- Verse 2
- Chorus
- Coda.

You might also use time code references to indicate where sections of the music begin or end, or to identify where particular musical features occur. If your composition or arrangement has been created using a music application that does not include standard music notation, you may wish to include some screenshots in your performance plan. If you do include screenshots, you must take care to explain what the screenshots represent in the music.

You can find examples of performance plan templates, with guidance notes, on the Bright Red Digital Zone.

ONLINE

Download examples of performance plan templates, with guidance notes, from www.brightredbooks.net/subjects.

AUDIO RECORDING

No matter what style or genre you have chosen for your composition or arrangement, you are required to submit an audio recording so that whoever is assessing your work can listen to it.

You may use any recording equipment available to you. However, in creating an audio recording, you must make sure that you choose an appropriate audio format for your final recording. You will need to be confident that anyone will be able to listen to it, irrespective of the device they are using to play it.

If you are using a specific music application to create your composition or arrangement, you may need to export your work to a universal file type, such as MP3, so that it will play on any device.

DON'T FORGET

Your composition or arrangement must have either a score or a performance plan, as well as an audio recording.

 THINGS TO DO AND THINK ABOUT

Once you have created your final audio recording, try playing it on more than one device to make sure that it will play back properly on any device. It would be advisable to try this at an early stage, even with an unfinished version of your composition or arrangement, just to make sure that everything works properly.

ASSIGNMENT

REVIEW OF THE CREATIVE PROCESS

In your review of the creative process of your composition or arrangement, you must provide a detailed account of:

- main decisions made
- exploration and development of musical ideas
- strengths and/or areas for improvement.

In the case of an arrangement, you should also make clear the details of your own creative input by providing details of what you have done to make your arrangement different from the original music.

The review should demonstrate that you have taken care to plan your composition or arrangement and that you have explored and developed musical ideas. You should refer specifically to the compositional methods you have used. And, finally, you should reflect on your work and provide specific examples of either the particular strengths of your composition or arrangement, or the areas that you think could be improved.

In reflecting on the strengths or areas for improvement, it is important that you relate your points specifically to the compositional methods used and how effectively you think you have developed them. General statements like: 'I think the music is effective' or 'I could have developed some of my ideas more' are not detailed enough.

Your review can be presented in prose or bullet points and should be approximately 200–350 words long. Short examples of music notation or screenshots may be included if they help to illustrate stages in your creative process. The suggested word count is given as a guide to the amount of evidence required. No penalty will be applied if you are outwith this word count.

DON'T FORGET

Your review must include a detailed account of main decisions made, exploration and development of musical ideas, and strengths and/or areas for improvement.

DON'T FORGET

For all three areas, you should provide a justification for your compositional choices.

WHAT A GOOD REVIEW LOOKS LIKE

The following table shows the three different areas that will be used in assessing your review. It also provides a summary of what would be good to include in your review, as well as some common faults that you should be trying to avoid.

Review of the creative process		
	What a good review might include	**Some common faults to be avoided**
Main decisions made	A detailed account of the main decisions made. This might include why you have chosen particular instruments, keys or time signatures, or certain melodic, harmonic or rhythmic features	A limited account of the main decisions made
	A clear explanation of how you planned your composition or arrangement. This might include referring to aspects of the texture, structure or form	Little evidence of planning

contd

Assignment: Review of the creative process

Exploration and development of musical ideas	A detailed account of the exploration and development of musical ideas. This might include how you have developed specific melodic, harmonic or rhythmic features	A limited explanation of the exploration and development of musical ideas
	Identifying clearly how you have used concepts	Simply listing concepts with little sense of how they have been used
	Indicating how you have experimented with compositional methods and developed your musical ideas	Little explanation as to how you have experimented with compositional methods or developed your musical ideas
	Showing that you have considered different possibilities	Little consideration given to different possibilities
	For an arrangement – clearly identifying details of your own creative input	For an arrangement – not identifying details of your own creative input
Strengths and/or areas for improvement	Clear identification of strengths and/or areas for improvement	Limited identification of strengths and/or areas for improvement
	Identifying clearly which musical ideas work well, and why they work well	Little reference as to which musical ideas work well, and why
	Identifying clearly which musical ideas do not work so well, and why they do not work so well	Little reference as to which musical ideas do not work well, and why

DON'T FORGET

Your arrangement must creatively rework the chosen music by exploring and developing musical ideas using all of the musical elements of melody, harmony, rhythm, structure and timbre.

MARKING CRITERIA

Your review will be awarded a mark out of 5, based on a range of summary statements. The following table shows a breakdown of the marks from 0 to 5, along with the related summary statements that will be used to assess your review.

Mark	Review of the creative process summary statements
5	The review contains: • a detailed account of the main decisions made • a detailed explanation of the exploration and development of musical ideas • clear details of strengths and/or areas for improvement.
4	The review contains: • a fairly detailed account of the main decisions made • a relevant explanation of the exploration and development of musical ideas • identification of strengths and/or areas for improvement.
3	The review contains: • a satisfactory account of the main decisions made • sufficient explanation of the exploration and development of musical ideas • satisfactory identification of strengths and/or areas for improvement.
2	The review contains: • a limited account of the main decisions made • a limited explanation of the exploration and development of musical ideas • limited identification of strengths and/or areas for improvement.
1	The review contains: • a poor account of the main decisions made • a very limited explanation of the exploration and development of musical ideas • little or no identification of strengths and/or areas for improvement.
0	No evidence produced

DON'T FORGET

For an arrangement, you must also make clear your own creative input.

DON'T FORGET

You must use the SQA review of the creative process template, which is available from the SQA Advanced Higher Music subject page.

ONLINE

You can find the review of the creative process templates, with guidance notes, by clicking the link on the Digital Zone at www.brightredbooks.net/subjects.

THINGS TO DO AND THINK ABOUT

Download the review of the creative process templates, with guidance notes, from the Digital Zone. Use the templates to collate details about:
- the main decisions you have made in planning your work
- the creative process, showing clearly how you have explored and developed musical ideas and used different compositional methods
- reflecting on your work, identifying what you consider to be the main strengths or areas for improvement.

ASSIGNMENT
ANALYSING MUSIC

Analysing music involves identifying the key features of a piece of music and demonstrating that you understand how the music works.

WHAT YOU NEED TO DO

You must choose a piece of music and analyse the key features with reference to compositional methods and music concepts. You cannot analyse your own music for this part of the assignment. Your analysis must include an audio recording of the piece of music you have chosen to analyse, either as an audio file or as a weblink to an online source. It is not necessary to provide edited excerpts of the audio recording. However, you should include audio time codes to clearly indicate where the key features you identify occur in the music. You may also include musical quotations from a score or a guide to the music referencing the key features you have identified.

CHOOSING MUSIC TO ANALYSE

In deciding on a piece of music to analyse, you might consider a piece of music or a song that you enjoy listening to. You might even choose something you have been performing, as you will probably have a good understanding of the music already.

It is important to choose a piece of music or song that has enough musical interest to provide sufficient scope for you to analyse. For example, suitable pieces of music to analyse might include:
- a popular or classical song, a song from a musical or an aria from an opera
- an instrumental piece such as sonata, suite or symphony

You should avoid choosing something that is too long, such as:
- a whole musical or opera or a complete song cycle
- a complete sonata, suite, symphony or concerto.

Having a copy of the sheet music or score for the music that you choose to analyse would also be beneficial. This would give you the opportunity to refer to aspects of the music notation as well as the audio recording.

Your analysis should focus on the key musical features and compositional methods used in the music and how effective they are. You should avoid simply listing or describing concepts without showing how they work in the music. You should also avoid too much biographical detail or background information, unless it is directly relevant to an understanding of the compositional methods used.

DON'T FORGET

Consider analysing a short piece of music or song that you are either performing or enjoy listening to.

WHAT A GOOD ANALYSIS LOOKS LIKE

This section outlines the characteristics of a good analysis, as well as the assessment criteria that will be used to award your analysis a mark out of 5.

The analysis of your chosen piece must identify key features within the music by referring to at least five of the following elements:

- style
- melody
- harmony
- rhythm and tempo
- texture
- structure and/or form
- timbre and dynamics.

The table lists these elements and provides a summary of what would be good to include in your analysis, as well as some common faults that you should try to avoid.

contd

92

Assignment: Analysing music

Analysis	What a good analysis should include	Some common faults to be avoided
Style	A perceptive understanding of the style with a valid justification given	Little reference to aspects of the style
Melody	Detailed identification of melodic features such as intervals, scales, ornaments or sequences	Little reference to, or understanding of, melodic features
Harmony	Detailed identification of harmonic features such as chords, inversions, cadences, keys, tonality or modulation	Little reference to, or understanding of, harmonic features
Rhythm and tempo	Detailed identification of rhythmic features such as tempo, time signatures, simple time, compound time, rhythmic groupings, triplets, augmentation or diminution	Little reference to, or understanding of, rhythmic features
Texture	Perceptive understanding of texture such as unison, octaves, accompanied, unaccompanied, homophonic or polyphonic/contrapuntal	Little reference to, or understanding of, texture
Structure and/or form	Perceptive understanding of structure and/or form such as binary, ternary, rondo, ritornello, sonata, strophic, through-composed, introduction or coda	Little reference to, or understanding of, structure and/or form
Timbre and dynamics	Perceptive understanding of instruments, voices, playing techniques such as arco, pizzicato, or con sordino, or features such as dynamics and accents	Little reference to, or understanding of, instruments, voices, playing techniques or dynamics
Overall	Detailed reference to the key features in the music, demonstrating a clear understanding of how the music works	Simply listing concepts or providing too much biographical detail or irrelevant background information

MARKING CRITERIA

Your analysis should be approximately 600–800 words long and will be awarded a mark out of 5 based on a range of summary statements. The following table shows a breakdown of the mark range from 0–5, along with the related summary statements that will be used to assess your analysis.

Mark range	Analysis summary statements
5	Demonstrating a perceptive understanding of the chosen piece by giving a detailed identification of key features of the music, backed up with detailed reference to the audio and, where appropriate, a score or guide to the music
4	Demonstrating a secure understanding of the chosen piece by giving a fairly detailed identification of key features of the music, backed up with fairly detailed reference to the audio and, where appropriate, a score or guide to the music
3	Demonstrating a satisfactory understanding of the chosen piece by giving a satisfactory identification of key features of the music, backed up with satisfactory reference to the audio and, where appropriate, a score or guide to the music
2	Demonstrating a limited understanding of the chosen piece by giving a limited identification of key features of the music, backed up with limited reference to the audio and, where appropriate, a score or guide to the music
1	Demonstrating little or no understanding of the chosen piece. There is little or no identification of key features of the music, backed up with little, inaccurate, or no reference to the audio nor, where appropriate, a score or guide to the music
0	No evidence produced

DON'T FORGET

You must provide an audio recording of the piece of music or song that you have chosen to analyse.

DON'T FORGET

You must use the SQA analysis template, which is available from the SQA Advanced Higher Music subject page.

DON'T FORGET

Download the analysis template, with guidance notes, from the Bright Red Digital Zone and use it to compile the key features you have identified.

THINGS TO DO AND THINK ABOUT

To develop your skills in analysing music, you should.
- Identify key features in the music under the headings of style, melody, harmony, rhythm and tempo, texture, structure and/or form, timbre and dynamics.
- Consider how effective these key features are in making the music work.

APPENDICES

GLOSSARY OF CONCEPTS

1st inversion See **Inversion**.

2nd inversion See **Inversion**.

5/4 time signature Five crotchet beats in every bar. This an example of an irregular time signature that does not fit into the pattern of either simple or compound time.

8va An abbreviation for the Italian term *ottava*, indicating that notes should be played an octave higher than written on the stave.

8vb An abbreviation for the Italian term *ottava bassa*, indicating that notes should be played an octave lower than written on the stave.

Added 6th A triad with the 6th note added above the root. For example, the three major triads of C, F and G, each contain three notes – the root, 3rd, and 5th. If the 6th note from the root is added above each triad this would create an **added 6th** chord, which is slightly richer and sweeter sounding and is often used in Jazz and other styles of popular music.

Air or **Ayre** A type of song commonly associated with Renaissance music. Commonly performed by a solo voice with instrumental accompaniment such as the lute or guitar.

Answer In a **fugue**, after the **subject** is heard at the beginning, the same theme is imitated by another voice part in the dominant key (a 5th higher or a 4th lower). This is called the **answer**. See **fugue, subject, countersubject,** and **stretto**.

Anthem A short sacred choral piece sung in English, regarded as the English equivalent of the Latin motet.

Antiphonal A texture involving more than one group of instruments or voices, using question and answer techniques. The groups are usually placed apart to create a stereo or spatial effect.

Appoggiatura Sometimes referred to as a *leaning note*, an **appoggiatura** is an ornamental note that comes either a step above or below the main note and resolves on to the main note.

Augmented 4th See **Tritone**.

Augmented triad A three note chord formed by altering a major triad by raising the 5th by a semitone, e.g. C, E and G sharp.

Ayre See **Air**.

Ballett A vocal piece for three to six voices, performed a cappella, associated with **Renaissance** music. The texture is generally homophonic, and the overall structure strophic. A noticeable feature is the use of a recurring "fa-la-la" refrain.

Bass clef C–E two ledger lines below stave to two ledger lines above The bass clef notes you need to know are from low C and D (below the stave) to high D and E (above the stave).

Bitonality The use of two different keys being used at the same time. See **Polytonality**.

Bridge A section of music that links two main themes. In popular music the **bridge** is a contrasting section that generally comes around the middle of a song.

Chorale A German hymn tune often harmonized for SATB with a homophonic texture.

Chord II A chord built on the second note of the scale. In a major key Chord II is a minor chord while in a minor key Chord II is a diminished chord. For example, in the key of C major chord II is the chord of D minor. In the key of A minor, Chord II is the chord of B diminished.

Chords I, IV, V and VI in major and minor keys Here are examples of chords based on the 1st, 4th, 5th, and 6th notes of the scale, in the keys of C major, G major, F major, and A minor:

Key	Chord I, V, IV and VI in the treble clef	Chord I, V, IV and VI in the bass clef
C major	C F G Am — I IV V VI	C F G Am — I IV V VI
G major	G C D Em — I IV V VI	G C D Em — I IV V VI
F major	F B♭ C Dm — I IV V VI	F B♭ C Dm — I IV V VI
A minor	Am Dm E F — I IV V VI	Am Dm E F — I IV V VI

Consort A small instrumental ensemble playing **Renaissance** music, often featuring recorders or viols.

Contemporary jazz A general term covering various styles of jazz music from about the 1980s onwards; including *jazz fusion* (a combination of jazz, rock, and funk), *pop jazz* (jazz interpretations of pop songs), *crossover* (including elements of rhythm and blues) and *smooth jazz* (a blend of jazz fusion and easy-listening pop). Common musical features include extended and chromatic improvisations, chromatic chords and discords, cross rhythms, syncopated rhythms, and riffs.

Countersubject In a **fugue**, after a voice has stated the **subject** or the **answer**, it continues with a new contrapuntal melody called the **countersubject**. See **fugue, subject, answer,** and **stretto**.

Countertenor A high adult male voice whose vocal range is higher than that of a tenor, being similar in range to that of a female alto or mezzo-soprano.

Creating a bass line using chord information provided Chord information will be provided in two ways: guitar chord symbols indicating if the chords are in root position (e.g. F, Gm, B♭, C or Dm), first inversion (1st Inv.) or second inversion (2nd Inv.), and Roman numerals indicating if the chords are in root position (e.g. I, II, IV, V or VI), first inversion (Ib, IIb, IVb, Vb or VIb) or second inversion (Ic, IIc, IVc, Vc or VIc).

Dal segno (D.S.) An Italian term (usually indicated by the abbreviation **D.S.**) indicating that the music should be repeated from a special sign.

Appendices: Glossary of Concepts

Diminished 5th An interval in which a perfect 5th is lowered by a semitone, e.g. C to G flat.

Diminished 7th A chord consisting of three intervals of a minor 3rd built one on top of the other, the interval between the lowest and highest note being a **diminished 7th**. For example, a **diminished 7th** based on B would contain the root (B), the minor 3rd (D), the diminished 5th (F), and the diminished 7th (A flat).

Dominant 7th A chord built on the dominant (5th) note of the scale and containing the root, 3rd, 5th, and 7th notes above the root. For example, in the key of C major the dominant 7th would start on the dominant note (G) and contain the notes G (root), B (3rd), D (5th), and G (7th).

EDM See **Electronic dance music**.

Electronic dance music (EDM) The term covers a range of styles popular since the 1980s, featuring sounds produced by synthesizers and drum machines, along with effects and processed samples from other recordings. It sounds electronic overall.

Enharmonic equivalent A note written in two different ways and called different names but sounding the same. For example, E flat can also be written as D sharp but both sound the same.

Fine An Italian term indicating the end of a piece of music. It is common for the abbreviation **D.S. (Dal segno)** to be combined with the term **Fine** to make the phrase **D.S. al Fine**. This instructs the performer to repeat from the sign and stop at the place marked **Fine**. See **Dal segno (D.S.)**.

Fugue A contrapuntal (or polyphonic) composition based on a single theme (called the **subject**) announced in one voice part alone, then imitated by other voices. Other features associated with **fugue** include **exposition, subject, answer, countersubject,** and **stretto**.

Galliard A **Renaissance** dance with three beats in a bar. A common features is use of a dotted crotchet-quaver-crotchet rhythm (♩.♪♩). It often follows a **pavan**.

Hemiola A rhythmic device giving the impression of the pulse changing from triple (3) time to duple (2) time, or vice versa.

Inversion 1. When a melodic phrase is turned upside down, creating a mirror image of the original phrase.

2 An inversion of a chord when a note other than the root is in the bass. If the root note is in the lowest the chord is said to be in root position. If the 3rd is the lowest note the chord is said to be in 1st inversion. If the 5th is the lowest note the chord is said to be in 2nd inversion.

Key signatures of D major, B flat major, E minor and D minor

The key signature of D major has two sharps (F sharp and C sharp):

The key signature of B flat major has two flats (B flat and E flat):

The key signature of E minor is the same as its relative major key of G major, and has one sharp (F sharp).

The key signature of of D minor is the same as its relative major key of F major, and has one flat (B flat).

See also **Scales of D major, B flat major, E minor and D minor**.

Leitmotif A recurring musical theme used to represent a person, place, emotion, object, or idea. The feature is associated with the operas of the Romantic composer Richard Wagner. However, the technique has also been used in orchestral music and film music.

Madrigal A vocal piece for three to six voices, performed a cappella, associated with **Renaissance** music. The texture is often polyphonic with much use of imitation, and the structure is often through-composed.

Motet A short sacred choral work with a Latin text, though not the same texts as a Mass, composed mainly for Catholic church services.

Nationalist A term used to describe music which incorporates elements of folk music, or is based on legends or folklore, of a particular country.

Neoclassical A style of music from the twentieth century in which large orchestral forces and complex textures were replaced by smaller ensembles and simpler textures. Some composers used forms and structures from earlier styles such as **Renaissance**, Baroque or Classical music, but still with a distinct 20th-century sound, often featuring abrupt modulations, unexpected melodic twists, and unusual harmonies.

Note row. See **tone row**

Pavan A **Renaissance** dance which generally has a slow to moderate tempo, with a feeling of either two or four beats in a bar. It is often followed by a **galliard**.

Piano trio A chamber group consisting of piano and two other instruments, usually a violin and a cello. The term can be used to describe both the group of performers that make up a **piano trio** and the piece of music composed for a **piano trio**.

Polytonality The use of two or more keys played or sung at the same time. See **bitonality**.

Renaissance A style of music from the middle of the fifteenth century to the end of the sixteenth century (i.e. between Medieval and Baroque). **Renaissance** music features both homophonic (chordal) textures, and polyphonic (contrapuntal) textures. Important types of **Renaissance** sacred music are the mass, **motet**, and **anthem**. Important vocal styles include the **madrigal**, **ballet** and **ayre** (or **air**). And popular dances include the **pavan** and **galliard**. It was common for **Renaissance** dances to be performed by an instrumental ensemble called a **consort**.

95

APPENDICES

Retrograde When the notes of a melody are played in reverse order. A common feature of **serial** music when the notes of a **tone row/note row** are used in reverse order. See **tone row/note row, retrograde** and **inversion**.

Rewriting (in either treble or bass clef) a note at the same pitch using up to two ledger lines below or above the stave

Here are notes A, B, C, D and E as they would be written at the higher end of the bass clef, using two ledger lines above the stave:

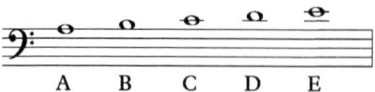

Here are the same notes written at the same pitch at the lower end of the treble clef, using two ledger lines below the stave:

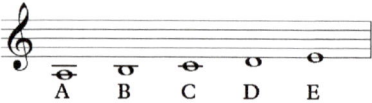

Scales of D major, B flat major, E minor and D minor

The scale of D major has two sharps (F sharp and C sharp).

The scale of B flat major has two flats (B flat and E flat).

There are two different kinds of minor scale: the *harmonic* minor and the *melodic* minor. The harmonic minor scale is the same both ascending and descending. The melodic minor scale, however, is not the same ascending and descending.

In the harmonic minor scale, the 7th note (or 7th degree of the scale) is raised by a semitone. This is the same whether the scale is ascending or descending. In the melodic minor scale, both the 6th and 7th notes are raised by a semitone when the notes are ascending, but are restored to their original pitch when the notes are descending.

The scale of E harmonic minor has an F sharp and a D sharp, both ascending and descending.

The scale of E melodic minor has an F sharp, C sharp and a D sharp in its ascending form. However, the 6th and 7th notes would be restored to C natural and D natural in the descending form.

The scale of D harmonic minor has a B flat and a C sharp, both ascending and descending.

The scale of D melodic minor has a B natural and a C sharp in its ascending form. However, the 6th and 7th notes would be restored to B flat and C natural in the descending form.

Examples of how these scales are notated can be found on pages 52 and 53.

See also **Key signatures of D major, B flat major, E minor and D minor**

Serial A method of composition from the twentieth century in which all twelve notes of the chromatic scale are organised into a fixed order called a **tone tow** or **note row**. This row can be transposed, inverted, or played in retrograde, and forms the basic musical material for an entire work or movement. See **tone row/note row, retrograde** and **inversion**.

Song cycle A selection of songs linked together using texts by the same writer or based on the same theme or subject, often outlining a story. Usually performed by voice and piano.

Sprechgesang A German term meaning *speech-song*. A technique in which the vocalist glides in and out of the written notes in a cross between singing and speaking.

Stretto A feature of a **fugue** in which the **answer** starts before the **subject** has finished, especially as a **fugue** progresses. See **fugue, subject, answer,** and **countersubject**.

Subject The main theme of a composition in sonata form such as a sonata, symphony, or concerto. Or the main theme on which a **fugue** is based. See **fugue, answer, countersubject,** and **stretto**.

Suspension A harmonic feature when a note from one chord is held over to the next chord creating a discord, which usually then resolves.

Syncopated rhythms Syncopation is a rhythmic feature where stronger accented notes are played on the weaker beats in a bar, or even between beats. For example, in 4/4 time the second beat might have the extra emphasis.

Ties A curved line which links two notes of the same pitch. It means that when the first note is sounded, it is held on for the combined value of both notes.

Time changes A change in time signature, such as from three beats in a bar to four beats in a bar, or from simple time to compound time.

Tone row or **note row** The arrangement of all twelve notes of the chromatic scale into a particular order and used as the basis for a composition. An important feature of **serial** music. The row can also be used in **inversion** or **retrograde**. See **serial, inversion** and **retrograde**.

Transposing from bass clef one octave higher into treble clef

Here are the notes A, B, C, D and E as they would be written at the higher end of the bass clef, using two ledger lines above the stave:

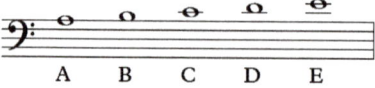

Here are the same notes transposed up one octave from the bass clef to treble clef:

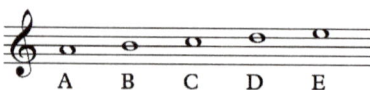

Tritone The interval of an augmented 4th, which is made up is made up of three whole tones.

Turn An ornament consisting of four notes which turn around a main note; starting with the note above, followed by the main note, then the note below, and returning to the main note. In music notation it is often indicted by a special symbol written above the music.